KV-576-852

Section 4: Language Fundamentals

Identify correctly constructed source files, `package` declarations, `import` statements, class declarations (of all forms including inner classes), `interface` declarations and implementations (for `java.lang.Runnable` or other interface described in the test), method declarations (including the `main` method that is used to start execution of a class), variable declarations and identifiers.

State the correspondence between index values in the argument array passed to a `main` method and command line arguments.

Identify all Java Programming Language keywords and correctly constructed identifiers.

State the effect of using a variable or array element of any kind when no explicit assignment has been made to it.

State the range of all primitive data types and declare literal values for `String` and all primitive types using all permitted formats, bases, and representations.

Section 5: Operators and Assignments

Determine the result of applying any operator, including assignment operators, `instanceof`, and casts to operands of any type, class, scope, or accessibility, or any combination of these.

Determine the result of applying the `boolean equals(Object)` method to objects of any combination of the classes `java.lang.String`, `java.lang.Boolean`, and `java.lang.Object`.

In an expression involving the operators &, |, &&, ||, and variables of known values, state which operands are evaluated and the value of the expression.

Determine the effect upon objects and primitive values of passing variables into methods and performing assignments or other modifying operations in that method.

continued in back ▶

Java 2

Exam Notes

Java™ 2
Exam Notes™

Philip Heller

San Francisco • Paris • Düsseldorf • Soest • London

Associate Publisher: Richard Mills

Contracts and Licensing Manager: Kristine O'Callaghan

Acquisitions and Developmental Editor: Denise Santoro Lincoln

Developmental Editor: Heather O'Connor

Editor: Susan Berge

Production Editor: Mae Lum

Technical Editor: John Zukowski

Book Designer: Bill Gibson

Graphic Illustrator: Tony Jonick

Electronic Publishing Specialist: Kris Warrenburg, Cyan Design

Proofreaders: Nelson Kim, Mae Lum

Indexer: Marilyn Smith

Cover Design: Archer Design

Cover Photograph: Photodisc

*I dedicate this work to
my goddaughter and her sister.*

—*Phil Heller*

Acknowledgments

Foremost gratitude to Kathryn, Max, and Harley. Thanks to my creative role models: Mom, Dave, Virginia, Melissa, and many more. Thanks to Gabriel, Alicia, y todos los salseros down at Alberto's. Thanks to Diane, Trish, and Troia at Sun for making sure that certification rocks. Thanks to Jason, Tanya, Cheryl, and Angie at Java U ... you're the best. In addition, thanks to the people at Sybex: Richard Mills, Denise Santoro Lincoln, Heather O'Connor, Susan Berge, Mae Lum, Kris Warrenburg, Nelson Kim, and Marilyn Smith.

—Phil Heller

Contents

Introduction

Passing the Sun Certified Java Programmer's Exam is the best possible way to establish your credentials as a Java programmer. It is also the prerequisite for more advanced certification exams from Sun and from other major high-technology companies.

The Programmer's Exam tests your knowledge of the basic Java language. It's a difficult exam, and passing it tells the world that you are able to make appropriate use of all aspects of the language.

Between these covers you will find a review of all the information you need to become a Sun Certified Java Programmer.

Is This Book for You?

The Sybex Exam Notes books were designed to be succinct, portable exam review guides. We designed this book primarily for Java programmers who are about to take the Sun Certified Java Programmer's Exam. You know who you are. This book is terse enough to serve as a memory aid and technical reminder of everything you need to know as you prepare for the exam. If you are unfamiliar with some of the concepts presented here, you may want to supplement your study with the *Complete Java 2 Certification Study Guide* (Sybex, 2000), by Simon Roberts, Philip Heller, and Michael Ernest. The Study Guide provides thorough explanations of concepts that this book assumes you are familiar with.

Our secondary audience is anybody who wants a handy reference guide for the ins and outs of the Java language. If you want to use this book for that purpose, we certainly won't stand in your way. In fact, we think it's a great idea.

How Is This Book Organized?

Sun publishes a list of specific exam objectives, the topics you need to master to pass the test. This book covers those objectives. For a complete list of the objectives, take a look inside the front and back covers of this book. Sun organizes the objectives into 10 groups. This book covers each group in a separate chapter. When you look at the contents of each chapter, you see how the chapters correspond to a group of Exam objectives, grouped and ordered in exactly the way Sun presents them. You also see that this book is definitely a review guide rather than an introduction to Java. Our main goal is to make it easy for you to determine which objectives you need to work on, and to learn more about those objectives.

As a result, some of the chapters are quite long, while others are quite short. In the publishing business there is a taboo against very long chapters, and even more so against very short chapters (like Chapter 3, "Garbage Collection," which we hope will set a world record for Shortest Chapter in a Java Book). We decided that if we didn't break a taboo or two, we couldn't present you with the best possible organization. Within each chapter, the individual exam objectives are addressed in turn. The following sections discuss each objective section in the book.

Critical Information

The "Critical Information" section presents the greatest depth of detail about the objective. This is where you'll find the explanations. It is tempting to say that this is where you'll find the meat of the chapter, but this book is published in California, so let's just say that this is where you'll find the protein of the chapter. This is the place to start if you're unfamiliar with or uncertain about the technical issues related to the objective.

Exam Essentials

In the "Exam Essentials" section you will find a concise list of the crucial topics that relate to the objective. You can scan this list to see if you need to review any topics.

Key Terms and Concepts

In the "Key Terms and Concepts" section you will find a mini-glossary of the most important terms and concepts presented in the chapter.

Sample Questions

The world is full of sample test questions for the Certified Java Programmer's Exam. Most of them have received mixed reviews at best. Naturally, we're fond of the sample questions that appear in the *Complete Java 2 Certification Study Guide*. Those questions closely resemble the real exam questions without giving anything away. They made you analyze code snippets, made you remember several things at once, kept you on your toes, tried to trip you up.

The questions in this book are completely different. Here the sample questions are much more focused. They are intended to make sure you are familiar with concepts that underlie the exam objectives. If you get tripped up, you can go back to the "Critical Information" section for another review. The important point is that these sample questions are not intended to look like the questions you will see on the real exam; the questions in this book are a tool for you to gauge what you need to study.

NOTE   Appendix A, "The Certification Initiative for Enterprise Development," discusses the alliance formed by Sun, IBM, Oracle, Novell, and Netscape to endorse Java certification.

Why Should You Get Certified?

Several reasons exist for why you might want to be certified, not least of which is that the certification is widely recognized as challenging and therefore demonstrates your possession of a good level of general competence in Java programming. Clearly at present, the number of Java jobs available exceeds the number of applicants, and this might make you think you won't gain much from certification. However, this is a non sequitur. Imagine yourself as a hiring manager, looking through a stack of resumes all applying for the highly desirable job you advertised. You have too many resumes to interview all applicants, so you must determine the criteria you will use to select the dozen or so applicants you actually invite to that crucial first meeting. Industry-recognized certification might well be a good criterion.

Beyond getting the job, or the promotion, you most want, is the matter of professional and personal confidence. Although the syntax of the Java programming language is much simpler than many other languages—certainly much simpler than C++—it is still a powerful and expressive language in which many elegant idioms thrive. The energy you expend in studying for the certification exams will give you a far more precise and complete understanding of the language, and with that understanding, you will gain a greater mastery of it and a greater confidence in yourself.

Last, and probably not least, is the matter of personal pride. Most good programmers are proud of their work and their skills. They get a warm feeling from looking at a particularly elegant piece of code and knowing that it is really well crafted—brief, accurate, and clean. But that pride might wane if, when your peers ask whether you're certified yet, you constantly have to answer with, "I can do this; I don't need to be certified." They'll be wondering, and so will you, if you're actually afraid of failure and if you're really as good as you think you are. After all, some people take the exam several times, getting better each time but still failing. It's not an exam that you pass simply by taking it. It's an exam you pass with blood, sweat, and tears. But that makes it all the more worthwhile.

Taking the Exam

You can take the Java Certification Exam whenever you like, by making an appointment with Prometric or Sun Educational Services. Prometric administers the exam on Sun's behalf; they have test centers throughout the world, so hopefully you won't have to travel far. The cost to take the exam is U.S.$150 (subject to change without notice).

NOTE The URL for Prometric is www.2test.com, and the URL for Sun Educational Services is http://suned.sun.com. Both sites provide phone numbers for contacting them.

You can make an appointment any time during regular business hours. You will be given 90 minutes and will probably need every minute to complete the approximately 60 questions on the exam. You will not be allowed to bring food or personal belongings into the test area. One piece of scratch paper is permitted; you will not be allowed to keep it after you have finished the exam. Many sites have security cameras.

You will be escorted to a cubicle containing a PC. The exam program will present you with questions selected from a pool. Navigation buttons take you to the next question or to previous questions for review and checking. When you have finished the test, the program will immediately present you with your score and a pass/fail indication. You will also be given feedback that indicates how well you performed in each of the dozen or so categories of the objectives. You will not be told which particular questions you got right or wrong.

Tips for Taking the Exam

There are no trick questions on the exam, but every question requires careful thought. The wording of the questions is highly precise; the exam has been reviewed not just by Java experts but also by language experts whose task was to eliminate any possible ambiguity. All you have to worry about is knowing Java; your score will not depend on your ability to second-guess the examiners.

In addition, it is not a good idea to second-guess the question layout. For example, do not be biased toward answer C simply because C has not come up recently. The questions are taken from a pool and presented to you in a random order. It is entirely possible to get a run of a particular option, but it is just as possible to get the answers evenly distributed.

Most of the questions are multiple choice. Of these, some have a single answer, while others require you to select all the appropriate responses. The Graphical User Interface of the test system indicates which kind of answer you should supply.

If a question only has one correct answer, you will be presented with radio buttons, so that selecting a second answer cancels the selection of a previous answer. With this kind of question, you have to select the most appropriate answer. If, on the other hand, you are presented with check boxes, you may need to make more than one selection, so every possible answer has to be considered on its own merits—not weighed against the others. You should be aware that where multiple answers are possible, you are being asked to make a decision about each answer, as though the question were five individual true/false questions. This requires more effort and understanding from you. In these cases, you are told how many answers to select; don't waste marks by ignoring this information. Think carefully, and always base your answer on your knowledge of Java.

The short-answer, type-in questions often cause undue concern. How are they marked? What happens if you omit a semicolon? These worries can stem from the knowledge that the questions are marked electronically and the belief that an answer might be marked wrong simply because the machine didn't have the sense to recognize a good variation of what it was programmed to accept. As with all exam questions, you should be careful to answer precisely what is asked. However, you should also be aware that the system does accept a variety of different answers; it has been set up with all the variations that the examination panel considered reasonable.

The test is taken using a windowed interface that can be driven almost entirely with the mouse. Many of the screens require scrolling; the scroll bar is on the right-hand side of the screen. Always check the scroll bar so you can be sure you have read a question in its entirety. It would be a shame to get a question wrong because you didn't realize you needed to scroll down a few lines.

The exam contains about 60 questions. On average, this gives you approximately a minute and a half per question. Some of the questions are easier than others, and undoubtedly there will be some that you can answer faster than others. However, you really do need to answer all the questions if you possibly can. The test system allows you to review your work after you reach the end. The system will explicitly direct your attention toward any multiple-choice questions that have no items selected. So, if you find a particular question difficult, consider moving on and coming back to it later.

If you pass, you will be given a temporary certificate. A few weeks later you will receive by mail a permanent certificate, along with whatever spiffs and gifts Sun is sending out at the time.

Getting your certificate is the official end of the process that began when you decided to take the exam. And, of course, it's really a beginning.

Conventions Used in This Book

This book uses several conventions to present information in as readable a manner as possible. Tips, Notes, and Warnings, shown below, appear from time to time in the text to call attention to specific highlights.

TIP This is a Tip. Tips contain specific programming information.

NOTE This is a Note. Notes contain important side discussions.

WARNING This is a Warning. Warnings call attention to bugs, design omissions, and other trouble spots.

This book takes advantage of several font styles. **Bold font** in text indicates something that the user types. A monospaced font is used for code, output, URLs, and file and directory names.

These style conventions are intended to facilitate your learning experience with this book—in other words, to increase your chances of passing the exam.

How to Contact the Publisher

Sybex welcomes reader feedback on all of its titles. Visit the Sybex Web site at www.sybex.com for book updates and additional certification information. You'll also find online forms to submit comments or suggestions regarding this or any other Sybex book.

Conventions Used in the Sun Certified Java Programmer's Examination* (Provided by Sun)

The Java Programmer's Examination includes the conventions described below. Some of them are intended to shorten the text that is displayed, therefore reducing the amount of reading required for each question. Other conventions help to provide consistency throughout the examination.

Conventions for Code

The code samples that are presented for you to study include line numbers. You should assume that the line numbers are not part of the source files, and therefore will not cause compilation errors.

Line numbers that begin with 1 indicate that a complete source file is shown. In contrast, if line numbers start with some other value, you should assume that the code you see is relevant to the question. You can assume that the omitted code would cause the code sample to compile correctly, and that it does not have any unexpected effects on the code in the question. So, for example, you should not choose an answer that says "The code does not compile" based only on the fact that you do not see a required import statement in the code sample that is presented.

In general, code of eight lines or less will be presented in the body of the question. If more than eight lines are needed, the code will be presented as an exhibit, and you will need to click the "Exhibit" button to see the code. Since you generally cannot see both the exhibited code and the question simultaneously due to limited screen size, you should read the question first, and use notepaper as necessary when considering an answer.

Conventions for Questions

When a question includes a code sample and asks "What is the result?" or something similar, you should consider what happens if you attempt to compile the code and then run it. This type of question admits the possibility that the code might not compile, or if it compiles, that it might not run. You should assume that all necessary support is given to the compilation and run phases (for example, that the CLASSPATH variable is appropriately set). Therefore, you should only examine possible causes of error in the information that is presented to you, and ignore information that is omitted.

Some of the possible answers use a form like this: "An error at line 5 causes compilation to fail." If you see this, you should consider whether the line in question is either a syntax error, or if it is inconsistent with some other part of the program and therefore misrepresents the program's clear intent. You should choose an answer of this type if the root of the problem is at the specified line, regardless of where any particular compiler might actually report an error.

Some questions might ask "Which answers are true?" or something similar. If an answer is worded like "An exception can be thrown," or "An exception may be thrown," then you should choose this answer if what it describes is possible, rather than disregarding it because the situation does not always occur. In contrast, if an option discusses something that "must" occur, then you should choose it only if there are no conditions under which the observation is untrue.

In multiple-choice questions that require you to pick more than one answer, you will be told how many options to choose, and the options will be presented as checkboxes. In questions that require you to pick only one answer, the possible answers will be presented with radio buttons that effectively prevent you from selecting more than one answer.

*Content provided from worldwide Web site http://suned.sun.com. Copyright © 1994-2000 Sun Microsystems Inc., 901 San Antonio Road, Palo Alto, CA 94303 USA. All Rights Reserved. Reprinted with permission.

Chapter
1

Declarations and Access Control

SUN CERTIFIED PROGRAMMER FOR JAVA 2
PLATFORM EXAM OBJECTIVES COVERED IN
THIS CHAPTER:

Write code that declares, constructs, and initializes
arrays of any base type using any of the permitted
forms both for declaration and for initialization.

Declare classes, inner classes, methods, instance
variables, static variables, and automatic (method
local) variables, making appropriate use of all permitted modifiers (such as *public, final, static,
abstract,* and so forth). State the significance of
each of these modifiers, both singly and in combination, and state the effect of package relationships on declared items qualified by these
modifiers.

For a given class, determine if a default constructor
will be created and, if so, state the prototype of
that constructor.

State the legal return types for any method, given
the declarations of all related methods in this or
parent classes.

The common theme of these four objectives is declaration. Declaration tells the compiler that an entity exists and also provides the name and nature of the entity. Since everything you create has to be declared, you must know how to declare correctly and be able to make appropriate use of all the declaration tools available to you. This objective recognizes the importance of declarations by requiring you to know everything about Java declarations.

Write code that declares, constructs, and initializes arrays of any base type using any of the permitted forms both for declaration and for initialization.

This objective addresses your understanding of all aspects of arrays. Arrays are the simplest possible data collection and are supported by all modern programming languages. However, Java's arrays are different from those in other languages, especially C and C++, because they are actually exotic objects. This objective recognizes the importance of being able to make use of all the functionality of arrays. You will be expected to know how to declare, construct, and initialize arrays.

Critical Information

You will need to know about the following aspects of arrays:

- Declaration
- Construction
- Initialization

These three steps are the first stages of an array's life cycle. The exam expects you to be familiar with all aspects of array declaration, construction, and initialization.

Array Declaration

Java supports two formats for array declaration. The first format is the classical C/C++ syntax, in which the element type comes first, followed by the variable name, followed by square brackets. This syntax is illustrated in line 1 as follows. The second format begins with the element type, which is followed by the square brackets and then by the variable name; the second format is illustrated in line 2 as follows.

```
1. int intarr[];
2. int[] intarr;
```

Array elements may be any of the following:

- Primitives (as shown previously)

- Object references

- References to other arrays

Declaration of arrays of primitives is illustrated in the preceding code. The following code shows the two ways to declare an array of object references:

```
1. String myStrings[];
2. String[] myStrings;
```

When an array's elements are references to other arrays, we have a special case of an array of object references. However, the declaration syntax is different from the syntax shown previously. The effect is like a multidimensional array, as shown in the following code. In line 3, the two declaration formats are combined, resulting in a declaration that is legal but difficult to read.

```
1. float[][][][] matrixOfFloats;
2. float matrixOfFloats[][][][];
3. float[][][] matrixOfFloats[];
```

Array Construction

Array declaration is like declaration of any other object reference variable. The declaration only tells the compiler about the type of the variable. No runtime object is created until new is invoked. Note that the declaration does not specify the number of elements in the array; the number of elements is supplied at runtime, as shown in the following examples:

```
 1. long longarr[];
 2. longarr = new long[10];
 3. String[] myStrings;
 4. myStrings = new String[22];
 5. double[][] matrixOfDoubles;
 6. matrixOfDoubles = new double[1152][900];
 7. int[][] matrixOfInts;
 8. matrixOfInts = new int[500][];
 9. matrixOfInts[0] = new int[33];
10. matrixOfInts[1] = new int[44];
```

Line 6 illustrates the most common way to construct the equivalent of a two-dimensional array. The matrixOfDoubles array looks like a 2-D array and can be treated as such. In reality it is an array of 1152 arrays of doubles. Each of those arrays of doubles has 900 elements. Line 8 constructs an array of 500 arrays of ints; those 500 arrays of ints are not yet allocated, and each of them may have a different length, as shown in lines 9 and 10.

Array Element Initialization

When an array is allocated, all of its elements are initialized. The initialization value depends on the type of array element, as shown in Table 1.1. The values are easy to remember because the numeric types are initialized to zero, and non-numeric types are initialized to values that are similar to zero. Also, these are the same values that are used for construction-time default initialization of an object's fields. The default for char is Unicode zero, which is the null character.

TABLE 1.1:   Array Element Initialization Values

Element Type	Initial Value
byte	0
short	0
int	0
long	0
char	'\u0000'
float	0.0f
double	0.0d
boolean	false
Object Reference	null

Declaration, Construction, and Initialization in a Single Statement

An array can be declared, constructed, and initialized in a single statement, as illustrated below:

```
double[] ds = {1.2, 2.3, 3.4, 4.5, Math.PI, Math.E};
```

With this syntax, the invocation of new and the size of the array are implicit. The array elements are initialized to the values given between the brackets, rather than their default initialization values.

Exam Essentials

Know how to declare and construct arrays.   The declaration includes one empty pair of square brackets for each dimension of the array. The square brackets can appear before or after the array name. Arrays are constructed with the keyword new.

Know the default initialization values for all possible types. The initialization values are zero for numeric type arrays, `false` for boolean arrays, and `null` for object reference type arrays.

Know how to declare, construct, and initialize in a single statement. This notation uses initialization values in curly brackets; for example, `int[] intarr = {1, 2, 3};`.

Key Terms and Concepts

Array declaration The square brackets in the declaration can appear before or after the variable name.

Default initialization values An array's elements are initialized to zero for numeric types and to values that resemble zero for non-numeric types, as shown in Table 1.1.

Sample Questions

1. Which of the following are legal array declarations?

   A. `int[] z[];`

   B. `String[][] z[];`

   C. `char[] z;`

   D. `char z[];`

   E. `float[5] z;`

   Answer: All the declarations are legal except E. You cannot specify an array's size in its declaration.

2. What are the default initialization values for an array of type `char`?

   Answer: '\u0000' (the null character). Table 1.1 lists initialization values for arrays of all primitive types.

3. What are the default initialization values for an array of type boolean?

Answer: false. Table 1.1 lists initialization values for arrays of all primitive types.

4. Which of the following are legal ways to declare, construct, and initialize an array in a single line?

A. char[3] cs = {'a', 'b', 'c'};

B. char[] cs = ['a', 'b', 'c'];

C. char[] cs = {'a', 'b', 'c', 'd'};

D. char cs[] = {'a', 'b', 'c', 'd'};

Answer: C and D are both legal. A is illegal because the array size is stated explicitly. B is illegal because it uses square brackets where curly brackets are required.

Declare classes, inner classes, methods, instance variables, static variables, and automatic (method local) variables, making appropriate use of all permitted modifiers (such as *public, final, static, abstract,* and so forth). State the significance of each of these modifiers, both singly and in combination, and state the effect of package relationships on declared items qualified by these modifiers.

This objective covers a lot of subject matter (and paper!). The big idea is modifiers. This section reviews Java's modifiers, including access modifiers, which relate to the phrase in the objective that mentions "the effect of package relationships."

It is possible to write Java programs that make little or no use of modifiers. However, appropriate use of modifiers—especially access modifiers—is essential for creating classes that are secure, object-oriented, and maintainable. This objective recognizes the importance of a working knowledge of Java's identifiers.

Critical Information

A *modifier* is a Java keyword that affects the behavior of the feature it precedes. (A feature of a class is the class itself, or a method, variable, or inner class of the class.) Java's modifiers are listed as follows:

- private
- protected
- public
- final
- abstract
- static
- synchronized
- transient
- native
- volatile

The first three of these modifiers (private, protected, and public) are known as *access modifiers*. The remaining modifiers do not fall into any clear-cut categories. (Another modifier, strictfp, is a new addition to Java 2. It is discussed briefly in Chapter 4, "Language Fundamentals," but does not appear on the exam.)

The Access Modifiers

There are four possible access modes for Java features: public, protected, default, and private. Three of these modes (public, protected, and private) correspond to access modifiers. The fourth mode (default) is the default and has no corresponding keyword modifier; a feature is default if it is not marked with private, protected, or `public`. Access modifiers generally dictate which *classes*, and not which *instances*, have access to features. You may use one access modifier at most to modify a feature. Automatic variables (that is, variables defined within the scope of a method or code block) may not take access modifiers.

The most restrictive access modifier is *private*. Only methods, data, and inner classes may be private; private classes are not permitted. A private method may only be called within the class that defines the method. A private variable may only be read and written within the class that defines the variable. A private inner class may only be accessed by the containing class; subclasses of the containing class may not access a private inner class. The granularity of private access is the class level, not the instance level: if a class has a private feature, then an instance of the class may access that private feature of *any instance* of the class.

"Default" is the default mode in the absence of a `private`, `protected`, or `public` modifier. This mode has no corresponding Java keyword. Classes, methods, and data may be default. A default class may be accessed by any class within its class's package. A default method of a class may be called from anywhere within the class's package. A default variable of a class may be read and written from anywhere within the class's package. A default inner class may be accessed by a subclass of the containing class, provided the containing class and the subclass are in the same package.

The *protected* access mode grants access permission to all members of the owning class's package, just as default access does. Moreover, additional access is granted if the class that owns a protected feature has a subclass in a different package. In this case an instance of the subclass may access protected data and call protected methods inherited from the parent instance. A protected inner class may be accessed by any subclass of the containing class, even if the subclass is in a different package from the containing class.

The most accessible access modifier is *public*. A public class may be accessed by any class. A public method may be called by any class (provided the calling class may access the class that owns the method in question). A public variable may be read and written by any class (provided the reading/writing class may access the class that owns the variable in question). A public inner class, like a protected inner class, may be accessed by any subclass of the containing class; moreover, public inner classes are a bit more available for manipulation via Java's reflection mechanism. The exact details are beyond the scope of the exam.

Table 1.2 summarizes Java's four access modes.

TABLE 1.2: Java's Access Modes

Access Mode	Java Keyword	Methods and Fields	Inner Classes
Private	`private`	Accessible only by owning class	Accessible only by owning class
Default	(no keyword)	Accessible by all classes in package of owning class	Accessible by same-package subclasses of enclosing class
Protected	`protected`	Accessible by all classes in package of owning class and by subclasses of owning class	Accessible by all subclasses of enclosing class
Public	`public`	Universal access	Accessible by all subclasses of enclosing class, plus some reflection

Table 1.3 shows which access modes are available to which feature types.

TABLE 1.3:   Features and Access Modes

Access Mode	Classes	Methods	Class Variables	Inner Classes
Private	NO	YES	YES	YES
Default	YES	YES	YES	YES
Protected	NO	YES	YES	YES
Public	YES	YES	YES	YES

Access and Packages

A package defines a namespace for classes: Every class within a package must have a unique name. Packages are hierarchical: A package may contain other packages. Package naming uses a period (.) to separate the components of a package hierarchy name. Thus, for example, the java package contains an awt subpackage, which in turn contains a subpackage called event. The fully qualified name of this last package is java.awt.event. Within this package is a class called AdjustmentEvent, whose fully qualified name is java.awt.event. AdjustmentEvent. No other class named AdjustmentEvent may exist in the java.awt.event package; however, it is legal for a class named AdjustmentEvent to exist in any other package.

One way to create a Java class that resides inside a package is to put a package declaration at the beginning of your source file. (Further details on package creation are not required knowledge for the Programmer's Exam and are beyond the scope of this book.) If you do not explicitly use a package declaration, a package might be implicitly created for you. At runtime, the Java environment creates a "default package" that contains all classes in the current working directory that do not explicitly belong to other packages.

Figure 1.1 shows a superclass, Parent, which is part of the packageA package. The Parent superclass has two subclasses. One subclass, childA, is also in the packageA package. The other subclass, childB, is in a different package, called packageB.

FIGURE 1.1: Package and subclass relationships

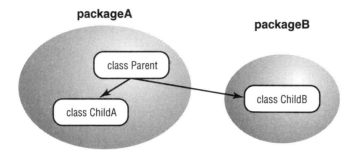

The childB subclass has access to all features of the Parent superclass that are public or protected. The childA subclass also has access to the public and protected features of Parent. In addition, since childA and Parent are in the same package, childA has access to all default features of Parent; this access would be the same if childA were not a subclass of Parent.

Default Access in Interfaces

In a class definition, the default access mode for a method is, of course, "default." This is not the case for a method in an interface. All interface methods are inherently public, so the default access mode for a method in an interface is public. Thus the following two interface versions are functionally identical:

```
Interface Inter {    // no access modifier
  double getWeight(Animal theAnimal);
}

Interface Inter {    // explicitly public
  public double getWeight(Animal theAnimal);
}
```

You are not allowed to apply any access modifier other than public to a method in an interface. The following interface generates a compiler error.

```
Interface BadAccess {
  protected double x();  // Compiler error
}
```

Access Examples

This section presents several examples of the use of access modifiers. All the examples refer to a simple class called packageA.Parent, which is listed below:

```
1. package packageA;
2.
3. public class Parent {
4.    private int     iPrivate;
5.    int             iDefault;
6.    protected int   iProtected;
7.    public int      iPublic;
8. }
```

The class definitions that follow illustrate each of the four Java access modes. All the code compiles; lines that illustrate illegal access attempts have been commented out.

The first example illustrates the private access mode. Since only the Parent class may access a private feature of the Parent class, our example is an expansion of Parent.

```
1. package packageA;
2.
3. public class Parent {
4.    private int     iPrivate;
5.    int             iDefault;
6.    protected int   iProtected;
7.    public int      iPublic;
8.
```

```
 9.    void xxx() {
10.       iPrivate = 10;              // My own
11.       Parent other = new Parent();
12.       other.iPrivate = 20;    // Someone else's
13.    }
14. }
```

Line 10 is an obvious use of the private access mode. The current instance of the Parent class is modifying its own version of iPrivate. Line 12 is less obvious: the current instance is modifying the iPrivate of a different instance of Parent. This example illustrates the principle that access modifiers grant access to *classes*, and not to *instances*.

The next example illustrates the default access mode, which grants access permission to all classes in the same package as the class that owns the default feature. Here we will create a second class in the packageA package.

```
 1.   package packageA;
 2.
 3.   public class InSamePackage {
 4.   void makeItSo() {
 5.      Parent parent = new Parent();
 6.      // parent.iPrivate = 10;
 7.      parent.iDefault = 20;
 8.      parent.iProtected = 30;
 9.      parent.iPublic = 40;
10.   }
11. }
```

Line 6 has to be commented out, because the attempted access to iPrivate in another class would not be allowed. Line 7 is legal because iDefault is a default variable in a class in the current package. Line 8 is legal because iProtected is a protected variable in a class in the current package. Line 9 is legal because iPublic is a public variable.

The next example illustrates the protected access mode, which grants access permission to all classes in the same package as the class that owns the protected feature, as well as to subclasses of the class that owns the feature. Here we will create a class in a second package, called packageB.

```
1. package packageB;
2.
3. public class InDifferentPackage
4.    extends packageA.Parent {
5.   void aMethod() {
6.       packageA.Parent parent =
             new packageA.Parent();
7.       // parent.iPrivate = 10;
8.       // parent.iDefault = 20;
9.       // parent.iProtected = 30;
10.      iProtected = 40;
11.      parent.iPublic = 50;
12.  }
13. }
```

Lines 7 and 8 have to be commented out for reasons that were illustrated in the previous examples. It may be surprising that line 9 does not compile and also must be commented out. The iProtected variable is protected; an instance of a subclass in a different package (such as the current instance of packageB.InDifferentPackage here) does not have access to the iProtected of every instance of packageA .Parent. Rather, an instance of the subclass may access the one instance of iProtected that the subclass instance inherits by virtue of extending Parent. The current instance of InDifferentPackage may access *its own* iProtected, as in line 10. Of course, line 11 compiles because it represents access to a public feature.

The last example in this section illustrates access and inner classes. Consider the following superclass:

```
1. package packageX;
2.
3. public class Parent {
4.    protected class Prot { public Prot() {} }
5. }
```

The superclass has a subclass in a different package:

```
6. package packageY;
7. import packageX.*;
8.
9. public class Child extends Parent {
10.    void xxx() {
11.       Prot p = new Prot();
12.    }
13. }
```

The Prot inner class is protected, so it is accessible from a subclass (Child in packageY) of the enclosing class (Parent in packageX), even though the parent and child classes reside in different packages. If the inner class were private or default, line 11 would not compile.

The Miscellaneous Modifiers

The remainder of this section examines the Java modifiers that have nothing to do with access. They are considerably simpler than the access modifiers. We will review each of the following keywords in turn:

- final
- abstract
- static
- native
- transient

- synchronized
- volatile

final

The final keyword conveys the sense that a feature may not be altered. Classes, methods, and variables may be final. A final class may not be subclassed, and a final method may not be overridden.

A final variable, once initialized, may not be written. The declaration and initialization of a final variable may appear in the same statement or in different statements. If they appear in different statements, those statements are not required to be consecutive, as illustrated in the following code sample:

```
final int j;        // Declare j
final int k = 10;   // Intervening statement
j = 20;             // Initialize Java
```

The final keyword, unlike the access modifiers, can be applied to the automatic variables and arguments of a method. A final automatic variable may not be written after it is initialized. A final argument may not be written at all. The following code sample illustrates final data in a method:

```
void aMethod(int x, final double z) {
  final char c = 'c';
  // etc.
}
```

abstract

The abstract keyword conveys the sense that a feature is somehow incomplete and cannot be used until further information is provided. Classes and methods may be final.

When you declare a method to be abstract, the class that contains the method has no definition for that method. Instead, the method definition is deferred to one or more subclasses. After the method name and parenthetical argument list, an abstract method has only a semi-colon, where a non-abstract method provides the method body enclosed in curly brackets. Subclasses provide the body of an abstract method.

An abstract class may not be instantiated. A class must be declared abstract if any of the following conditions apply:

- The class contains one or more abstract methods.

- The class does not provide an implementation for each of the abstract methods of its superclass.

- The class declares that it implements an interface, and the class does not provide an implementation for each method of the interface.

The following code illustrates abstract classes.

```
1. abstract class Parent {
2.    abstract void x(int a);
3. }
4.
5. class ChildA extends Parent {
6.    void x(int a) {
7.       System.out.println("a = " + a);
8.    }
9. }
10.
11. class ChildB extends Parent {
12.    void x(int a) {
13.       System.out.println("I did it my way" + a);
14.    }
15. }
16.
17. abstract class ChildC extends Parent { }
```

The class Parent must be declared abstract on line 1, because it contains an abstract method. The classes ChildA and ChildB do not have to be abstract, since they provide implementations for the parent class's abstract method. Class ChildC on line 17 does have to be abstract, since it does not provide an implementation for its parent's abstract method.

static

Data and methods may be declared static. Static features belong to the class in which they are declared, rather than belonging to individual instances of that class.

A class's static variable is allocated and initialized when the owning class is loaded. A class's static variable may be referenced via a reference to any instance of the owning class, or via the name of the class itself. For example, suppose class C has a static variable v. If Cref1 and Cref2 are references to instances of class C, then the static variable can be referenced as C.v, Cref1.v, or Cref2.v.

A method that is declared static must observe the following restrictions:

- The static method may only access those variables of its owning class that are declared static; the class's nonstatic variables may not be accessed.

- The static method may only call those methods of its owning class that are declared static; the class's nonstatic methods may not be called.

- The static method has no this reference.

- The static method may not be overridden.

It is legal for a class to contain static code that does not exist within a method body. Such code is known as *static initializer* code; it is executed when the owning class is loaded, after static variables are allocated and initialized. Static initializer code has no this reference. The code listed below illustrates a static initializer:

```
1. public class StaticDemo {
2. static int i=5;
3.
4.    static { i++; }
5.
6.    public static void main(String[] args) {
```

```
7.        System.out.println("i = " + i);
8.    }
9. }
```

When the application is started, the StaticDemo class is loaded. During the class loading process, the static variable i is allocated and initialized to 5. Later in the class loading process, i is incremented to 6. When the main() method executes, it prints out "i = 6".

synchronized

The synchronized modifier applies only to code. The modifier requires a thread to acquire a lock before executing the code. This topic is covered in Chapter 7, "Threads."

transient, native, volatile

The keywords transient, native, and volatile modify features in ways that are beyond the scope of the Programmer's Exam. They are covered briefly here, because the exam only requires you to be aware of their syntax.

The transient modifier applies only to class variables. During serialization, an object's transient variables are not serialized.

A native method calls code in a library specific to the underlying hardware. A native method is like an abstract method in the sense that the implementation exists somewhere other than the class in which the method is declared. The following code illustrates the syntax of a native method; note the semicolon in the place where an ordinary method would have a method body enclosed in curly brackets:

```
native int callnat(char c, String s);
```

The volatile modifier applies only to class variables. Volatile data is protected from certain kinds of corruption under multithreaded conditions.

Exam Essentials

Understand the four access modes and the corresponding keywords. You should know the significance of public, default, protected, and private access when applied to data, methods, and inner classes.

Understand how Java classes are organized into packages, so that you can understand the default and protected modes. A package is a namespace containing classes. You should know how the default and protected modes grant access to classes within the same package.

Know the effect of declaring a final class, variable, or method. A final class cannot be subclassed; a final variable cannot be modified after initialization; a final method cannot be overridden.

Know the effect of declaring an abstract class or method. An abstract class cannot be instantiated; an abstract method's definition is deferred to a subclass.

Understand the effect of declaring a static variable or method. Static variables belong to the class; static methods have no this pointer and may only access static variables and methods of their class.

Know how to reference a static variable or method. A static feature may be referenced through the class name or through a reference to any instance of the class.

Be able to recognize static initializer code. Static initializer code appears in curly brackets with no method declaration. Such code is executed once, when the class is loaded.

Key Terms and Concepts

Abstract class An abstract class may not be instantiated.

Abstract method An abstract method contains no body, deferring definition to non-abstract subclasses.

Default class   A class with default access may be accessed by any class in the same package as the default class.

Default inner class   A default inner class may be accessed from the enclosing class and from subclasses of the enclosing class that reside in the same package as the enclosing class.

Default method   A method with default access may be called by any class in the same package as the class that owns the default method.

Default variable   A variable with default access may be read and written by any class in the same package as the class that owns the default variable.

Final class   A final class may not be subclassed.

Final method   A final method may not be overridden.

Final variable   A final variable, once initialized, may not be modified.

Private inner class   A private inner class may only be accessed from the enclosing class.

Private method   A private method may only be called by an instance of the class that owns the method.

Private variable   A private variable may only be accessed by an instance of the class that owns the variable.

Protected inner class   A protected inner class may be accessed by the enclosing class and by any subclass of the enclosing class.

Protected variable and protected method   Protected access expands on default access by allowing any subclass to read and write protected data and to call protected methods, even if the subclass is in a different package from its superclass.

Public class, protected variable, and protected method   Public access makes a feature accessible to all classes without restriction.

Public inner class   A public inner class has the same access as a protected inner class and can be more manipulated by reflection.

Static initializer   Static initializer code executes during class-load time, after static variables are allocated and initialized.

Static method A static method may only access the static variables and methods of its class.

Static variable Static data belongs to its class, rather than to any instance of the class. Static variables are allocated and initialized at class-load time.

Sample Questions

1. Which of the following are access modifiers?

A. abstract

B. final

C. private

D. protected

E. public

F. static

G. synchronized

Answer: C, D, and E. The other modifiers are not access modifiers. The fourth access mode, "default," has no corresponding modifier keyword.

2. If class ClassY has private method z(), can an instance of ClassY call the z() method of a different instance of ClassY?

Answer: Yes. A private feature may be accessed by any instance of the class that owns the feature.

3. Which access mode is more restricting: default or protected?

Answer: Default. Protected access is default plus some subclass access.

4. Can a static method write a nonstatic variable of the class that owns the static method?

Answer: No. A static method can only access the static data and methods of its class.

5. Can a non-abstract class contain an abstract method?

Answer: No. A class that contains any abstract methods must itself be declared abstract.

6. Which of the following statements are true?

A. A final method may be overridden.

B. A final method may not be overridden.

C. A final class may be subclassed.

D. A final class may not be subclassed.

Answer: B and D. Final methods may not be overridden, and final classes may not be subclassed.

For a given class, determine if a default constructor will be created and, if so, state the prototype of that constructor.

This objective requires you to know about Java's behind-the-scenes constructor behavior. This objective is important because most classes have to be instantiated to be useful, and instantiation means invoking a constructor.

Critical Information

A *default constructor* is a constructor with an empty argument list. For example, the default constructor for a class named MyClass would have the following format:

```
MyClass() { ... }
```

Every class must have at least one constructor. If you create a class that has no explicit constructors, then a default constructor is automatically generated by the compiler. In this case, the access mode of the constructor depends on the access mode of the class. If the class is public, the automatically generated constructor is also public. If the class is not public, the automatically generated constructor has default access. (Access is slightly different for inner classes, but this level of detail is not covered on the exam.)

Exam Essentials

Know that the compiler generates a default constructor when a class has no explicit constructors.   When a class has constructor code, no default constructor is generated.

Know the access mode of the generated constructor.   Public for public classes; default for classes with any other access mode.

Key Term and Concept

Default constructor   A constructor with an empty argument list.

Sample Questions

1. What is the prototype for the automatically generated constructor of the following class?

```
public class Kat extends Mammal { }
```

Answer: `public Kat()`. Automatically generated constructors always have empty argument lists. For a public class such as this one, the automatically generated constructor is public.

2. Does the compiler automatically generate a constructor for the following class?

```
Class Kat extends Mammal {
    Float weight;
    Kat(float f) { weight = f; }
}
```

Answer: No. The class has an explicit constructor, so the compiler does not automatically generate a default constructor.

State the legal return types for any method, given the declarations of all related methods in this or parent classes.

This objective concerns certain aspects of overloading and overriding. These are essential concepts in object-oriented programming, and the exam recognizes their importance in this objective and in the objectives covered in Chapter 6 ("Overloading, Overriding, Runtime Type, and Object Orientation").

You will be expected to know Java's rules for method overloading and overriding. The rule for access of overridden methods has already been discussed (in the section of this chapter that covers the long objective that begins "Declare classes..."). Here we will review the other factors that relate to overloading and overriding.

Critical Information

Overloading is reuse of a method name within a class. *Overriding* is reuse of a method name in a subclass.

To determine the legality of an attempt to overload or override a method, consider three things:

- The method's name

- The method's argument list

- The method's return type

Method Overloading

Overloaded methods share a common name but have different argument lists. Overloaded methods may have the same or different return types. Thus, within a single class the following methods may appear and are examples of legal overloading:

```
1. void aaa(int i, double d) { ... }
2. private String aaa(long z) { ... }
3. String aaa(long z, double d) { ... }
```

These three methods have the same name and different argument lists. The access modes and return types are irrelevant.

If a class contains the three methods shown previously, then it would be illegal to add the following method into that class:

```
4. double aaa(long z, double d) { ... }
```

The new method has the same name and argument list as the method on line 3, so it is illegal even though it has a different return type.

Method Overriding

When a method is overridden, the version in the subclass must match the name, argument list, and return type of the version in the superclass. Compilation fails if the subclass version has the same name and argument list as the superclass version but has a different return type.

Compilation succeeds if the subclass version has the same name as the superclass version but has a different argument list, whether or not the return type is different. However, this is not really method overriding; it is overloading of the method inherited from the superclass.

Exam Essentials

Know the legal return types for overloaded and overridden methods. There are no restrictions for an overloaded method; an overriding method must have the same return type as the overridden version.

Key Terms and Concepts

Overloading Reuse of a method name within a class. The methods must have different argument lists and/or return types.

Overriding Reuse of a method name in a subclass. The subclass version must have the same name, argument list, and return type as the superclass version.

Sample Questions

1. If two methods in a single class have the same name and different argument lists, can they have different return types?

Answer: Yes. As long as the argument lists are different, the overloading is legal.

2. Is it legal for two methods in a single class to have the same name and the same argument list, but different return types?

Answer: No. Two methods in a class may not have the same name and argument list.

3. When is it legal for a method to have the same name and argument list as a method in the superclass?

Answer: If the two methods have the same return type, then we have an example of legal overriding. If the return types are different, the code will not compile.

Chapter

2

Flow Control and Exception Handling

SUN CERTIFIED PROGRAMMER FOR JAVA 2 PLATFORM EXAM OBJECTIVES COVERED IN THIS CHAPTER:

- Write code using *if* and *switch* statements and identify legal argument types for these statements.

- Write code using all forms of loops including labeled and unlabeled use of *break* and *continue* and state the values taken by loop control variables during and after loop execution.

- Write code that makes proper use of exceptions and exception handling clauses (*try, catch, finally*) and declare methods and overriding methods that throw exceptions.

Java's flow-control mechanisms include the classical if, switch, and loop constructs that are familiar to all C and C++ programmers, as well as the more modern exception handling mechanism. All these mechanisms have nuances not found in other languages. This group of objectives requires you to have a full understanding of Java's flow control.

Write code using *if* and *switch* statements and identify legal argument types for these statements.

This objective covers Java's non-looping flow control. Even the simple if and switch statements have nuances that make them slightly different from their corresponding C and C++ statements. You will be tested for a thorough knowledge of if and switch.

Critical Information

The argument of an if statement must be of boolean type. The following code illustrates legal and illegal if statements:

```
int x = 100;
if (x != 0) { ... } // Legal
if (x)      { ... } // Illegal
```

The switch statement takes an argument that must be of type byte, short, char, or int. (These are the types that can be automatically converted to int, according to the principles that will be reviewed in the first part of Chapter 5, "Operators and Assignments.")

The following code illustrates correct use of the switch statement:

```
 1. void aMethod(int z) {
 2.   switch(z) {
 3.     case 0:
 4.       System.out.println("CASE 0");
 5.       break;
 6.     case 1:
 7.       System.out.println("CASE 1");
 8.     case 2:
 9.       System.out.println("CASE 2");
10.       break;
11.     default:
12.       System.out.println("CASE OTHER");
13.       break;
14.   }
15. }
```

The 0 case is the most common form. After line 4 executes, the break statement on line 5 causes control to break out of the switch block. The 1 case has no break statement, so control falls through into the code for the 2 case. The default code, if present, handles all cases that are not explicitly covered by case statements. Table 2.1 shows this example's output for various input cases.

TABLE 2.1: switch Statement Output

Value of Z	Output
0	CASE 0
1	CASE 1
	CASE 2
2	CASE 2
Any other value	CASE OTHER

Exam Essentials

Know the legal argument types for if and switch statements.   The argument of an if statement must be of type boolean. The argument of a switch must be of type byte, short, char, or int.

Recognize and create correctly constructed switch statements. You should be able to create regular and default cases, with or without break statements.

Key Terms and Concepts

Argument of an if statement   Must be boolean.

Argument of a switch statement   Must be byte, short, char, or int.

Sample Questions

1. Which of the following Java types are legal arguments for an if statement?

A. byte

B. short

C. int

D. long

E. float

F. double

G. boolean

H. char

I. Object reference

Answer: G. boolean is the only legal argument type for an if statement.

2. Which of the following Java types are legal arguments for a `switch` statement?

A. `byte`

B. `short`

C. `int`

D. `long`

E. `float`

F. `double`

G. `boolean`

H. `char`

I. Object reference

Answer: A, B, C, and H. The only legal types are `byte`, `short`, `char`, and `int`.

Write code using all forms of loops including labeled and unlabeled use of *break* and *continue* and state the values taken by loop control variables during and after loop execution.

This objective tests your knowledge of Java's various forms of loop.

Critical Information

Java supports three forms of loop:

- `while` loops

- do loops

- `for` loops

Each of these forms offers the standard loop behavior that is familiar to C and C++ programmers, as well labeled break and continue functionality.

while Loops

The general form of the while loop is as follows:

```
while (boolean_condition)
  <repeated_code>
```

The argument that follows the while statement must be of boolean type. The condition is tested first; if it evaluates to true then the repeated code is executed. The condition is then tested again, and the process continues, as shown in Figure 2.1. It is possible that the repeated code will not be executed.

FIGURE 2.1: while loop flow

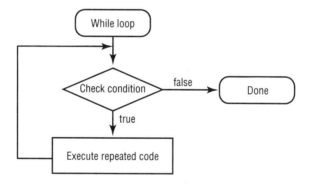

do Loops

The general form of the do loop is as follows:

```
do
  <repeated_code>
while (boolean_condition)
```

As with while loops, the argument that follows the while statement must be of boolean type. However, with do loops, the repeated code is always executed at least once. The condition is tested after the repeated code executes, as shown in Figure 2.2.

FIGURE 2.2: do loop flow

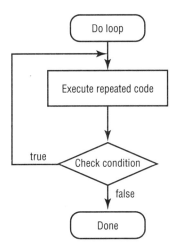

for Loops

The general form of the for loop is as follows:

```
for (<init> ; <boolean_condition> ; <iteration>)
    <repeated_code>
```

Three expressions appear in parentheses after the for keyword: an initialization statement, a boolean condition, and an iteration statement. First the initialization statement is executed; this only happens once. The looping behavior consists of repeatedly testing the boolean condition and, if the condition is true, executing first the repeated code and then the iteration statement. The initialization and iteration expressions are allowed to be empty, as is the repeated code. The behavior of a for loop is shown in Figure 2.3.

FIGURE 2.3: for loop flow

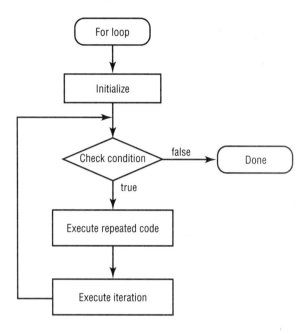

break and *continue*

All three loop versions (while, do, and for) support breaking and continuing.

NOTE The break keyword appears in the context of loops and also in the context of switches. The meaning of break is very different in these two cases.

For all three kinds of loop, **break** means immediately terminate loop execution, and proceed with the code that immediately follows the loop. Loop conditions are not reevaluated; in a for loop, the iteration code is not executed before termination.

For all three kinds of loop, `continue` means immediately terminate the current pass through the loop, and proceed with the next pass (unless, of course, the current pass is the last pass). Treatment of loop control code depends on the type of loop, as listed below.

`while` loop   Reevaluate condition (at beginning of loop code). If condition is true, pass through the loop again; otherwise loop is finished.

`do` loop   Reevaluate condition (at end of loop code). If condition is true, pass through the loop again; otherwise loop is finished.

`for` loop   Reevaluate condition (at beginning of loop code). If condition is true, pass through the loop again and execute iteration statement; otherwise loop is finished. The exam objective requires you to know the value of a loop-control variable at the end of the loop. The following code illustrates the behavior of each kind of loop, executing 10 times.

```
int x = 0;
while (x < 10) {
  // Loop work would go here
  x++;
}
System.out.println("x = " + x);

int y=0;
do {
  // Loop work would go here
  y++;
}
while (y < 10);
System.out.println("y = " + y);

int z = 0;
for (z=0; z<10; z++) {
  // Loop body would go here
}
System.out.println("z = " + z);
```

The output of this code fragment is as follows:

```
x = 10
y = 10
z = 10
```

This example shows that each control variable increments 10 times. Be aware that breaking out of a loop may or may not cause control variables to increment, depending on the kind of loop.

Java supports *labeled break* and *labeled continue* loops. A *label* is an identifier, followed by a colon, that comes before the while, do, and for keyword of a loop. No other construct may be labeled. A labeled break has the format

```
break <a_label>;
```

A labeled continue has the format

```
continue <a_label>;
```

The labeled break and continue must appear within a loop that is labeled with a_label. They are useful in nested loop situations, when code in an inner loop wants to cause a break or continue of an outer loop. They cause the break or continue to happen in the loop specified by the label, rather than the current loop. For example, the following code calls aMethod() for all combinations of x and y except the case where x = 5 and y >= 6.

```
Outer: for (int x=0; x<10; x++) {
  for (int y=0; y<10; y++) {
    if (x==5 && y==6)
      continue outer;
    aMethod(x, y);
  }
}
```

The following code calls anotherMethod() for all combinations of x and y, until x and y are both 7; at that point the loop is finished.

```
Outer: for (int x=0; x<10; x++) {
  for (int y=0; y<10; y++) {
    if (x==7 && y==7)
      break outer;
    anotherMethod(x, y);
  }
}
```

Exam Essentials

Understand the operation of Java while, do, and for loops.   You should be able to construct each kind of loop and know when blocks are executed and conditions evaluated.

Understand labeled loops, labeled breaks, and labeled continues in the context of while, do, and for loops.   Know how flow control proceeds in each of these structures.

Key Terms and Concepts

Break   Terminate execution of the current loop.

Continue   Terminate the current pass through the current loop.

Label   An identifier for a loop.

Labeled break   Terminate execution of the labeled loop.

Labeled continue   Terminate the current pass through the labeled loop.

Sample Questions

1. Which of the following kinds of loop always execute at least one pass?

A. do loops

B. for loops

C. while loops

Answer: A. Only do loops execute the loop body before testing the condition. for loops and while loops test the condition before executing the loop body.

2. In the code listed below, what value is printed out at line 9?

```
1. int w = 0;
2. outer: for (int x=0; x<5; x++) {
3.    for (int y=0; y<100; y++) {
4.      if (x == 3)
5.        break outer;
6.      w++;
7.    }
8. }
9. System.out.println("w = " + w);
```

Answer: 300. The inner loop increments w 100 times when x is 0, then 100 times when x is 1, and then another 100 times when x is 2. After that the test in line 4 is true, so the outer loop breaks and no more incrementing takes place.

Write code that makes proper use of exceptions and exception handling clauses (*try, catch, finally*) and declare methods and overriding methods that throw exceptions.

The exception handling mechanism is a relatively modern addition to programming language functionality. Exceptions provide an elegant way to abnormally return from a method and to react to the abnormal return. Good exception programming results in maintainable code. This objective recognizes the importance of exceptions.

Critical Information

You will need to know about the following aspects of Java's exception functionality:

- Checked exceptions
- The try/catch mechanism
- Declaring methods that throw exceptions
- The finally option
- Throwing exceptions
- Exceptions and overriding

We will review each of these aspects in turn. Without a thorough understanding of all of them, you will not be able to take full advantage of Java's powerful exception capability. The exam expects you to be completely competent in all aspects of exception programming.

Checked Exceptions

Checked exceptions are exception types that are not java.lang
.RuntimeException or its subclasses. java.lang.RuntimeException
and its subclasses are known as *runtime exceptions,* as shown in Figure 2.4.

FIGURE 2.4: Exception class hierarchy

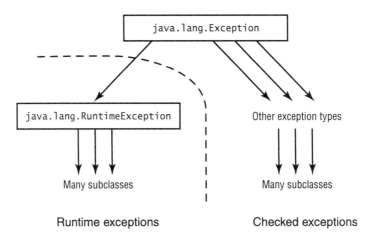

All of the exception handling mechanisms described in the upcoming
sections are mandatory for code that throws checked exceptions and
optional for code that throws runtime exceptions. Checked exceptions generally depict conditions that are beyond the programmer's
control, such as undesirable I/O status. Runtime exceptions connote
undesirable conditions that are completely within the programmer's
control, such as an array index being out of bounds. Thus, runtime
exceptions are appropriately dealt with because the programmer
writes code that ensures the exceptions will never occur.

The Try/Catch Mechanism

An exception can be intercepted with the try/catch mechanism. Code
that throws checked exceptions is surrounded by curly brackets prefixed by the try keyword. The try block is followed by one or more
catch blocks, and then optionally by a finally block. (The catch

blocks are optional if a `finally` block is present; this situation is discussed in the upcoming section on the `finally` keyword.) The following code example attempts to create a file reader and an instance of the `Class` class. The constructor on line 2 throws `IOException`.

```
1. try {
2.    FileReader fr = new FileReader("a");
3.    Class c = Class.forName("AClassName");
4. }
5. catch (FileNotFoundException fnfx) {
6.    System.out.println(fnfx.getMessage);
7. }
8. catch (ClassNotFoundException cnfx) {
9.    System.out.println(cnfx.getMessage);
10. }
```

The `FileReader` constructor call on line 2 throws `FileNotFound-Exception`; the `Class.forName()` method on line 3 throws `FileNot-FoundException`. Both exception types are checked exceptions (as opposed to runtime exceptions). There is one exception handler for each type.

If an exception is thrown from the `try` block (lines 2 and 3), then the current pass through the block is abandoned, and execution proceeds in the appropriate `catch` block. To determine which `catch` block is appropriate, the JVM considers the exception type of each block in turn, checking whether the exception that was thrown is an instance of, or a subclass of, the exception type of the block. So, for example, if line 5 were modified to catch `IOException` (which is a superclass of `FileNotFoundException`), the `catch` block on lines 5–7 would still catch a `FileNotFoundException` thrown by the constructor call on line 2.

When an exception is thrown from a `try` block, only one `catch` block is executed. After the `catch` block executes, control continues at the code immediately following the last `catch` block.

Declaring Methods that Throw Exceptions

If you want to write code that throws checked exceptions, there is an alternative to putting the code in a try block: you can declare that the method containing the code throws the exception types. For example, all three lines of the method listed below call a method that throws IOException. The exceptions are dealt with by having the method itself declare that it throws IOException.

```
1. void writeEcks(String fname) throws IOException {
2.   FileReader fr = new FileReader(fname);
3.   fr.write('x');
4.   fr.close();
5. }
```

Every exception type thrown in the body of the method (except those types explicitly caught in catch blocks) must be the same class as, or a subclass of, one of the exception types thrown by the method.

The *finally* Option

A try block may optionally be followed by a finally block, which must come after the last catch block. If a finally block is present, it will be executed no matter what happens in the try block. In other words, the finally block will execute whether or not an exception is thrown and, if an exception should be thrown, no matter how that exception is handled.

The only circumstances that can prevent full execution of a catch block are catastrophic: death of the current thread or of the JVM, failure or power-off of the CPU, or calling System.exit(). The code example of the previous section is modified below to use a finally block, which prints out a message whether or not an exception is thrown.

```
1. try {
2.   FileReader fr = new FileReader("a");
3.   Class c = Class.forName("AClassName");
4. }
5. catch (FileNotFoundException fnfx) {
```

```
 6.    System.out.println(fnfx.getMessage);
 7. }
 8. catch (ClassNotFoundException cnfx) {
 9.    System.out.println(cnfx.getMessage);
10. }
11. finally {
12.    System.out.println("In finally block.");
13. }
```

A finally block is useful when one or more exception types are thrown from the try block and not caught by any catch block. Such exceptions must be declared as thrown by the method in which the try block appears, as discussed in the previous section.

It is legal to have a try block that has no catch blocks and is followed by a finally block. In this case all checked exceptions thrown from the try block must be declared as thrown by the current method. If an exception is thrown, the current method's finally block executes; then the exception is handled by the calling method's handler.

Throwing Exceptions

Throwing exceptions is accomplished with the throw keyword, followed by a reference to an instance of Exception. Since (of course) the throw statement initiates an exception, it must appear either in a try block or in a method that declares that it throws the exception. When you construct exceptions, be aware that most exception classes in the core Java API have at least two constructors: a default constructor and a form that takes a String argument. The String argument version is preferred; the argument can be retrieved from the exception by calling getMessage(). The following example shows a method that throws a DataFormatException.

```
public void check1stChar(String s)
throws DataFormatException {
  if (s == null)
    return;
  char c = s.charAt(0);
```

```
      if (c != '+' && c != '-')
throw new DataFormatException("Bad 1st char: " + c);
}
```

Exceptions and Overriding

When you override a method that throws checked exceptions, the subclass version is allowed to throw exceptions, provided that every checked exception type thrown by the subclass version is the same as, or a subclass of, a checked exception type thrown by the superclass version.

For example, consider the exception class hierarchy shown in Figure 2.5.

FIGURE 2.5: Example of exception class hierarchy

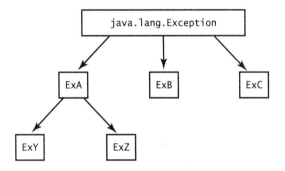

Suppose class ParentClass has a method called aMethod() that throws exceptions ExA and ExB. If you extend ParentClass and attempt to override aMethod() in the subclass, then the subclass's version of the method is allowed to throw any of the exception types listed below. (The method is also allowed to throw no exceptions at all.)

- ExA
- ExB
- ExY
- ExZ

Exam Essentials

Understand the difference between checked exceptions and runtime exceptions.   Know the inheritance of these families of exception types, and know which kinds must be explicitly handled in your code.

Analyze code that uses a try block, and understand the flow of control no matter what exception types are thrown.   You should be completely familiar with all the functionality of the try, catch, and finally blocks

Understand all of your exception handling options when calling methods that throw checked exceptions.   You should know how to create try blocks and how to declare that a method throws exceptions.

Know what exception types may be thrown when you override a method that throws exceptions.   You need to be familiar with the required relationships between the superclass version's exception types and the subclass version's exception types.

Key Terms and Concepts

catch block   A block of code that follows a try block and handles one specific exception type and its subclasses.

Checked exception   An exception type other than RuntimeException and its subclasses. Checked exceptions must be handled using the techniques reviewed in the "Checked Exceptions" section.

finally block   A block of code that follows a try block and all its catch blocks. A finally block is (almost) always executed, no matter what exception is thrown or where the exception is handled.

Runtime exception   An exception that is an instance of RuntimeException or one of its subclasses. Runtime exceptions may be handled using the techniques reviewed in "The Try/Catch Mechanism" section, but such handling is optional.

try block. A block of code, prefixed with the try keyword, that might throw an exception.

Sample Questions

1. Suppose Axn and Bxn extend IOException. Suppose you want to override a method whose signature is void xyz() throws IOException. Which of the following declarations are legal for your overriding method?

   A. void xyz() throws Axn

   B. void xyz() throws Axn, Bxn

   C. void xyz() throws Axn, IOException

   D. void xyz() throws Axn, Exception

   E. void xyz() throws Exception

   Answer: A, B, C. Any exceptions that are thrown from the overriding method must be IOException or subclasses of IOException.

2. Which of the following statements are true?

   A. Runtime exceptions must be caught.

   B. Runtime exceptions may be caught but do not have to be.

   C. Checked exceptions must be caught.

   D. Checked exceptions may be caught but do not have to be.

   Answer: B, C. Checked exceptions must be caught; runtime exceptions may be caught.

Chapter

3

Garbage Collection

SUN CERTIFIED PROGRAMMER FOR JAVA 2 PLATFORM EXAM OBJECTIVE COVERED IN THIS CHAPTER:

- State the behavior that is guaranteed by the garbage collection system and write code that explicitly makes objects eligible for collection.

Y ou should be conversant with the mechanisms of the garbage collection system and with the ways your programming interacts with it.

Garbage collection simplifies the programmer's job enormously. Memory management is susceptible to two types of error—memory can be used simultaneously for two purposes, or it can remain unavailable for reuse after it is no longer needed. Both of these errors can cause major problems for any program. An automatic garbage collection system such as Java provides prevents the first of these problems and reduces but does not eliminate the second.

State the behavior that is guaranteed by the garbage collection system and write code that explicitly makes objects eligible for collection.

T his objective is intended to ensure you have a clear grasp of the responsibilities that rest with you as the programmer. It also ensures you understand the control—and lack of control—you have over the allocation and deallocation of memory. Proper handing of available memory is a crucial concern for anyone writing commercial grade applications, because memory is a finite resource in any computer system and forcing a program to resort to virtual memory will slow it down dramatically.

Critical Information

Two types of errors can occur in memory management in general programming: Memory can be made available for reuse while it is actually still in use, and memory that is no longer in use can remain allocated and unavailable for reuse.

Java's garbage collection system entirely prevents accidental releasing of memory: As long as an object is accessible from any live thread, the object will remain valid, and the memory associated with it will not be reused. The garbage collector guarantees that it will not reclaim memory that is still in use or is potentially still usable.

There are two types of memory leak, which we shall call hard leaks and soft leaks. They are similar, but Java's memory management system only helps with the hard leak. A *hard leak* occurs in languages without a garbage collection system, when there are no references to an area of memory, but that area of memory has not been released. The area of memory is then permanently lost from the program. This type of leak cannot occur with Java, since the scenario described, having zero references to an area of memory, is the definition of how the garbage collector decides the area is eligible for collection.

The second type of leak, a *soft leak*, occurs when a program has areas of memory that the program will never again use but that have not been, and will not be, released. Java's garbage collection cannot protect against soft leaks because to do so would require semantic understanding of the meaning and operation of the algorithms that are being coded, and that represents artificial intelligence at a level beyond the skills of modern programming.

To avoid soft memory leaks with Java, simply write null into any reference that will not be used again. The object will become eligible for garbage collection as soon as all references to it are either set to null or become inaccessible.

When a local variable goes out of scope, it becomes inaccessible and therefore is no longer a valid reference to an object. Thus, it doesn't explicitly require setting to null.

Limitations of the Garbage Collector

When the garbage collector runs, it consumes a certain amount of CPU time. Depending upon the particular garbage collection algorithm used in any given JVM, the rest of the JVM might be frozen while the collection proceeds.

The garbage collection system runs in a thread of its own. Since the thread scheduling algorithm is not specified by Java, you cannot know when, or if, the thread will run. Generally, of course, in the absence of high priority runnable threads, the garbage collector will get its turn. However, the uncertainty surrounding thread scheduling is one of the main reasons there are no guarantees about when, or even if, the garbage collector will reclaim memory. Even calling System.gc() or Runtime.gc() does not force the garbage collector to run.

If the JVM starts to run short of memory, the garbage collector will be set running before an out-of-memory error occurs. This does not happen if the system is running short of system resources, such as file handles, network sockets, or windows. This is the purpose of the dispose() method of the Window class and the close() method of the stream classes.

In general, the limitations of the garbage collector can be summed up as follows: No promises are made regarding when, how fast, or even if the garbage collector will recover a given unreferenced object from memory.

Exam Essentials

Understand memory reclamation and the circumstances under which memory will be reclaimed. If an object is still accessible to any live thread, that object will certainly not be collected. This is true even if the program will never access the object again—the logic is simple and cannot make inferences about the semantics of the code. No guarantees are made about reclaiming available memory or the timing of reclamation if it does occur. In a standard JVM, there is no entirely reliable, platform-independent way to force garbage collection.

Understand `System.gc()` and `Runtime.gc()` and their effects on garbage collection.   The `gc()` methods in the `System` and `Runtime` classes make it more likely that garbage collection will run but do not guarantee it; for example, other threads might retain the CPU.

Recognize the significance of writing `null` into a variable.   Simply abandoning a variable and allowing it to retain its reference value is likely to cause wasted memory, since any valid reference prevents an object from being garbage collected. To indicate to the runtime system that a reference is no longer in use, thereby making it possible for an unused object to be collected, assign `null` into a variable to delete the old reference. Of course, writing `null` does not of itself make the object collectable; that occurs only when no more accessible references exist.

Key Terms and Concepts

Live reference   A reference that is accessible to a live thread.

Live thread   A thread that has been started but has not yet died.

Memory leak   An area of memory that will not be used by the program but that will not be reclaimed for reuse. Java only partially protects against this problem. Write `null` into references you have finished with to help yourself.

Referenced memory   Memory that is being used for storage of an object that is accessible by a live reference.

`Runtime.gc()`   `gc()` is a static method in the `java.lang.Runtime` class. By calling the method, you request that the garbage collector run. However, calling the method does not guarantee that the garbage collector will run, nor does it guarantee any limiting timescale in which the garbage collector might run.

`System.gc()`   Another way to request garbage collection, with the same limitations as `Runtime.gc()`.

Unreferenced memory   Memory that is not being used for storage of any object accessible by a live reference.

Sample Questions

1. Which memory management problems are addressed by garbage collection?

A. Accidental deallocation of memory that is still in use

B. Failure to reclaim all unneeded memory

C. Failure to reclaim inaccessible memory

D. Insufficient physical memory

E. Insufficient virtual memory

Answer: A, C. Memory cannot be accidentally deallocated; any live reference prevents this. Inaccessible memory is precisely what the garbage collector looks for, so C is true. However, unneeded memory that is still accessible by a live reference will not be collected and will waste space, so B is false. Similarly, if there is insufficient memory, either physical or virtual, the garbage collector cannot help. Either the program will fail due to insufficient virtual memory, or the virtual memory system will thrash if there is insufficient physical memory.

2. Which is true?

A. Calling `System.gc()` causes garbage collection to occur, but the time for the process to complete is unspecified.

B. Calling `Runtime.gc()` causes garbage collection to occur, but the time for the process to complete is unspecified.

C. Memory leaks are impossible in Java.

D. Memory is used more efficiently in Java.

E. Memory corruption due to double use of memory is impossible in Java.

Answer: E. Calling gc() in either of its guises does not guarantee that the garbage collector will run, so A and B are false. Memory leaks can happen if you fail to null out accessible references to unneeded memory. Memory is not used any more efficiently, so D is false. However, double use of memory is impossible, since accessible memory is never returned to the heap for reuse, so it cannot be accidentally reallocated.

3. What is the effect of calling System.gc()?

   A. Garbage collection occurs immediately.

   B. Garbage collection occurs but not necessarily immediately.

   C. Garbage collection might occur soon, if other system behavior permits.

   Answer: C. As the documentation notes, calling the gc() method "suggests" that the system expend effort to run the garbage collection system. So, only C is true.

4. In the following program, which of the objects can be released at point X on line 10 (assuming there is further behavior between line 10 and the program's exit)?

```
1. public class Test {
2.     private Object o = new Object();
3.     private static final Object p = new Object();
4.
5.     public static void main(String [] args) {
6.         Test t = new Test();
7.         Test u = new Test();
8.         t.o = null;
9.         method(u);
10.        // point X, other behavior follows
11.    }
12.
13.    public static void method(Object u) {
14.        Object q = new Object();
```

```
15.      u = null;
16.    }
17. }
```

A. Variable o in Test object t

B. Variable p in the Test class

C. Variable o in Test object u

D. Variable q in the method method()

E. Variable t in the method main()

F. Variable u in the method main()

Answer: A, D. Because line 8 writes null into the member variable t.o, and t.o was the only reference to that object, it becomes collectible immediately after line 8, making A true. Variable p is static and final, so as long as the class is loaded, the target of the reference cannot be collected. In the code, variable u at line 7 is left unchanged, as is member o. Therefore, C is false since the object remains accessible at least until line 10. At line 16, when the method method() returns, the local variable q goes out of scope, and the object it refers to becomes unreferenced. Therefore, D is true. Although member t.o is set to null at line 8, the variable t is not nulled out; therefore the object it refers to cannot be collected, and E is false. In lines 13 and 15, a local variable called u is declared and nulled out; however, this is a second reference to the object that variable u declared at line 7. Therefore, even though it is set to null at line 15, a live accessible reference remains at line 10, making F false.

Chapter

4

Language Fundamentals

SUN CERTIFIED PROGRAMMER FOR JAVA 2 PLATFORM EXAM OBJECTIVES COVERED IN THIS CHAPTER:

- Identify correctly constructed source files, package declarations, import statements, class declarations (of all forms including inner classes), interface declarations and implementations (for *java.lang.Runnable* or other interface described in the test), method declarations (including the main method that is used to start execution of a class), variable declarations and identifiers.

- State the correspondence between index values in the argument array passed to a main method and command line arguments.

- Identify all Java programming language keywords and correctly constructed identifiers.

- State the effect of using a variable or array element of any kind when no explicit assignment has been made to it.

- State the range of all primitive data types and declare literal values for *String* and for all primitive types using all permitted formats, bases, and representations.

he objectives in this group are concerned with program structure and with very low-level entities: keywords, identifiers, arrays, primitives, and literals. These topics are not especially glamorous or fascinating, but they are the bottom-level building blocks out of which all programs are made. These objectives emphasize the importance of being familiar with all the lowest-level details of the Java language.

Identify correctly constructed source files, package declarations, import statements, class declarations (of all forms including inner classes), interface declarations and implementations (for *java.lang .Runnable* or other interface described in the test), method declarations (including the *main* method that is used to start execution of a class), variable declarations and identifiers.

The first objective of this chapter covers several subjects. The common theme is that you will be tested on your ability to recognize correctly constructed elements of a Java program. This ability is vital, because a program with even a single incorrectly constructed element will not compile.

Critical Information

This objective covers a broad range of topics that concern various aspects of correctly constructed Java source code. The topics are as follows:

- Source file structure
- Package declarations
- Import statements
- Class declarations
- Inner classes
- Interface declarations and implementations
- Method declarations
- The main() method
- Variable declarations
- Identifiers

Without a thorough understanding of these topics, you cannot create source code that compiles correctly. The sections that follow discuss each of these topics in turn except for identifiers, which are the subject of their own objective and are covered later in this chapter.

Source File Structure

At the coarsest level of detail, a Java source file is a collection of *compilation units*. A compilation unit is a package declaration, an import statement, or a class or interface definition. Within a source file, compilation units must appear in the following order:

1. Package declarations
2. Import statements
3. Class and interface definitions

None of the compilation units is mandatory. The next three sections examine the three kinds of compilation units.

Package Declarations

A package declaration has the following structure:

```
package packagename;
```

Packages may contain subpackages to any arbitrary depth. This is analogous to directories, which may contain subdirectories, which may in turn contain their own subdirectories. The fully qualified name of a package consists of a dot-separated list of the containing packages, starting with the outermost package. For example, suppose you create a source file that contains several class definitions, and you want all the classes to reside in a package called parser, which resides in a package called stained_glass_software, which in turn resides in a package called com. Your package declaration would be as follows:

```
package com.stained_glass_software.parser;
```

If a source file contains no package declaration, the classes and interfaces defined in the file will be placed in the default unnamed package.

Import Statements

Every class and interface belongs to a package. If a source file does not contain a package declaration, then its classes and interfaces are placed in a special default package.

If a class belongs to a package other than the default package, then the complete name of the class is the full package name, followed by a period, followed by the class name. The same principle holds for interface names. Thus, for example, the complete name of the DragSource class in the java.awt.dnd package would be java.awt.dnd.DragSource. Using the complete long class name is a terrible inconvenience. Consider the following declaration and construction:

```
java.awt.dnd.DragSource src = new
java.awt.dnd.DragSource();
```

If we had to use complete class names all the time, programming in Java would be extremely clumsy. Fortunately, the import statement provides a way to abbreviate class and interface names.

A basic import statement consists of the import keyword, followed by a full class name (dot-separated package and class name), followed by a semicolon:

```
import package_name.class_name;
```

The import statement tells the compiler that all occurrences in the source file of "class_name" should be replaced with "package_name.class_name". Thus, the import statement allows you to use the short class name as an abbreviation for the full class name. Both class names and interface names can be abbreviated in this way.

A second form of the import statement allows you to import all classes and interfaces in a package:

```
import package_name.*;
```

This statement imports all classes and interfaces in the specified package; however, classes and interfaces in subpackages within the package are not imported. Only one star (*) may appear on an import line, and it must appear at the end of the statement, just before the semicolon.

Class Declarations

This section reviews declarations of top-level classes. The exam requires you to be familiar with both top-level and inner classes. Inner classes are discussed in Chapter 6, "Overloading, Overriding, Run-time Type, and Object Orientation."

The syntax of a top-level class declaration is as follows:

```
<modifiers> class <classname>
[extends <superclassname>]
[implements <interfaces>] {<class_definition>}
```

Modifiers may appear in any order. The legal modifiers for top-level classes are as follows:

- `public`
- `abstract`
- `final`
- `strictfp`

Chapter 1, "Declarations and Access Control," discusses the meaning of all except the last of these modifiers. The `strictfp` keyword was introduced in Java 2 and can be applied to classes, interfaces, and methods. It controls floating-point behavior under certain specific circumstances.

The [`extends` `<superclassname>`] phrase is optional; if it is omitted, the class extends `java.lang.Object`. The [`implements` `<interfaces>`] phrase is also optional. A class may implement multiple interfaces; in this case, the `implements` keyword appears only once, followed by a comma-separated list of interface names. A class must be declared `abstract` if it does not provide an implementation for every method of every interface that the class declares it implements.

NOTE   It is illegal to declare a class to be both `abstract` and `final`. Such a class would be of little use, since only its non-abstract subclasses could be instantiated, and subclasses would be illegal.

The code that constitutes the definition of the class appears between the curly brackets that follow the class's name. A class definition is a sequence of any number of the following kinds of building block:

- Variable declaration
- Method declaration
- Constructor declaration
- Initializer

- Static initializer

Variable, method, and constructor declarations are covered in subsequent sections. Initializers and static initializers are reviewed here.

An *initializer* is a block of code, enclosed in curly brackets, that is not part of a method body. The following code shows an example of an initializer.

```
class A {
  int x, y, z;
  {
    x = 100;
    y = 200;
    z = 300;
  }
}
```

When an instance of a class is created, all initializers are executed before constructor execution. Thus, in the class discussed above, any constructor can expect x, y, and z to be correctly initialized.

A *static initializer*, like an ordinary initializer, is a block of code, enclosed in curly brackets, that is not part of a method body; however, a static initializer's opening curly bracket is prefixed by the keyword static. A class's static initializers are executed when the class is loaded, after static data is allocated. A static initializer has access to all static data and methods of its class.

Static initializers are useful when initialization of a static variable requires multiple statements. For example, the Socket constructor throws IOException, so the following class code will not compile:

```
1. class X {
2.    static Socket s = new Socket("ruby", 5432);
3. }
```

The initialization has to take place in a static initializer, as follows.

```
1. class X {
2.    static Socket s;
3.    static {
4.       try {
5.          s = new Socket("ruby", 5432);
6.       }
7.       catch (IOException x) { }
8.    }
9. }
```

The static initializer appears from line 3 through line 8.

Interface Declarations and Implementations

An interface declaration has the following form:

```
[public][strictfp] interface <interface_name>
   [extends <superinterfaces>] {<interface_body>}
```

The public modifier is optional; its significance was discussed in Chapter 1. The strictfp modifier is also optional; other modifiers are not allowed. Unlike a class, an interface may extend multiple superinterfaces; if this is the case, the extends keyword appears only once, and the superinterface names are separated by commas. If interface Inter extends one or more superinterfaces, and class AClass declares that it implements Inter, then AClass must provide an implementation for every method of Inter, and also for every method of the superinterfaces. If AClass does not provide all those implementations, then AClass must be declared abstract.

An interface body consists of method declarations and constants. All methods and constants in an interface are public. Explicitly declaring them public is allowed but redundant; attempting to apply any other access modifier results in a compiler error. All methods of an interface are abstract; explicitly declaring them abstract is allowed but redundant. The Java Language Specification discourages the use of redundant explicit pubic and abstract declarations in interfaces.

A method declaration in an interface is like an abstract method declaration in an abstract class: the method body is absent. A semicolon appears in place of the curly-bracket-enclosed method body. The format of an interface method declaration is as follows:

```
[public] [abstract] <return_type> <method_name>
(args_list);
```

An interface is allowed to contain definitions of constant data. All data defined in an interface is public, final, and static.

The following code shows an example of an interface that extends multiple superinterfaces and contains method declarations and data.

```
1. public interface AnInterface extends If1, If2 {
2.    int i = 101;
3.    float f = 12.34f;
4.    double getAltitude();
5.    String getID(boolean flag);
6. }
```

Since AnInterface is an interface, the variables declared on lines 2 and 3 are implicitly public, final, and static; the methods declared on lines 4 and 5 are implicitly public and abstract.

The objective specifically mentions the java.lang.Runnable interface. This interface defines a single method:

```
void run(Runnable r);
```

Thus, a class that declares that it implements Runnable must either declare itself as abstract or provide a method as follows:

```
public void run() { <method body> }
```

The Runnable interface is an essential part of thread programming, which is discussed further in Chapter 7.

Method Declarations

A method declaration commonly has the following format:

```
[modifiers] <return_type> <method_name>
(<args_list>)
   [throws <exceptions_list>] { <method_body> }
```

The modifiers and the "throws" clause are optional. Modifiers may appear in any order. With this format, the following modifiers are permitted:

- Access modifiers (`public`, `protected`, or `private`)
- `final`
- `static`
- `synchronized`
- `strictfp`

This format is used when a method declaration appears in conjunction with the method's body. There are two cases in which the method's body does not appear with its declaration:

- Abstract methods
- Native methods

The format of abstract and native methods is as follows:

```
[modifiers] <return_type> <method_name>
(<args_list>)
   [throws <exceptions_list>];
```

Here one of the modifiers is of course abstract or native. Note the semicolon at the end of the declaration, where the method body would normally appear. Again, modifiers may appear in any order.

Constructors are (or resemble, depending on your interpretation) methods with certain restrictions. The method name is always the name of the current class. There is no return type, since the constructor returns a reference whose type is the current class. Thus the format of a constructor is as follows:

```
[modifiers] <current_class_name> (<args_list>)
[throws <exceptions_list>]
  {<constructor_body>)
```

Once again, the modifiers may appear in any order.

The *main()* Method

The main() method is the entry point for all applications. The declaration of the main() method is as follows:

```
public static void main(String[] args) {
  <method_body>
}
```

The args argument reflects the application's command-line arguments. Command-line arguments are the subject of a separate objective, which is covered later in this chapter.

Variable Declarations

A variable declaration has the following format:

```
[modifiers] <variable_name> [= <initial_value>];
```

Modifiers are optional. The following modifiers are allowed to modify variables:

- Access modifiers (public, protected, or private)
- final
- static
- transient
- volatile

The modifiers may appear in any order. The one modifier whose functionality is not covered on the exam is volatile, which protects multithreaded shared data from being put at risk by optimizing compilers. The volatile modifier is not considered reliable.

Exam Essentials

Recognize and create correctly constructed source files. You should know the various kinds of compilation units and their required order of appearance.

Recognize and create correctly constructed declarations. You should be familiar with declarations of packages, classes, interfaces, methods, and variables.

Key Terms and Concepts

Import An import statement tells the compiler to allow the abbreviation of a fully qualified class name.

Initializer A block of code, enclosed in curly brackets, that is not part of a method. A class's initializers are executed just before constructor execution.

main() method The entry point for an application.

Static initializer A block of code, enclosed in curly brackets and prefixed with the `static` keyword, that is not part of a method. A class's static initializers are executed when the class is loaded.

Sample Questions

1. Which of the following is/are valid interface declarations? (Assume X, Y, and Z are interfaces.)

   A. `public interface A extends X {void aMethod();}`

   B. `interface B implements Y {void aMethod();}`

   C. `interface C extends X, Y, Z {void aMethod();}`

   D. `interface C extends X {protected void aMethod();}`

Answer: A and C. A is a straightforward interface. B is illegal because an interface may not implement another interface. C is legal because an interface is permitted to extend multiple super-interfaces. D is illegal because all interface methods are public, so the method may not be declared protected.

2. How many lines does the following application print out?

```
1. public class Q2 {
2.    {System.out.println("Hello.");}
3.
4.    public static void main(String[] args) {
5.       new Q2(); new Q2(); new Q2();
6.    }
7. }
```

A. 0

B. 1

C. 2

D. 3

E. 4

Answer: D. The initializer on line 2 is executed every time the class's constructor is invoked. Since the constructor is invoked three times, three lines of output are generated.

3. How many lines does the following application print out?

```
1. public class Q2 {
2.    static {
3.       System.out.println("Hello.");
4.    }
5.
6.    public static void main(String[] args) {
7.       new Q2(); new Q2(); new Q2();
8.    }
9. }
```

A. 0

B. 1

C. 2

D. 3

E. 4

Answer: B. The static initializer on lines 2–4 is invoked once, when the class is loaded. Thus the code outputs a single line.

4. Does the following class compile without error?

```
1. class X implements Runnable {
2.   public void run(Runnable r) { }
3. }
```

A. Yes

B. No

Answer: B. The Runnable interface contains the method void run(), which takes no arguments. The method on line 2 does not satisfy the interface, so the compiler fails. The error message states that class X must be declared abstract, because it does not fully implement the Runnable interface.

State the correspondence between index values in the argument array passed to a main method and command line arguments.

This objective makes sure you know how to make an application access the arguments that the user enters on the command line that invokes the application.

Critical Information

The main() method is the entry point for an application. When you invoke an application from the command line, a Java Virtual Machine (JVM) is created. Then the JVM loads the class that you specified on the command line and calls the class's main() method. The main() method has the following declaration:

```
public static void main(String[] args) { ... }
```

Since modifiers may appear in any order, the following declaration is legal and equivalent:

```
static public void main(String[] args) { ... }
```

However, the return type is not considered a modifier, so the following declarations are illegal:

```
static void public main(String[] args) { ... }
void public static main(String[] args) { ... }
```

A class is allowed to have a main() method that does not match the required declaration, such as the following:

```
public static int main(String[] args) { ... }
```

However, such a main() method will not be called when the class is invoked as a method.

An application with *n* command-line arguments is invoked as follows:

```
java [<command_line_options>] Application_Class_Name
    arg1 ... argn
```

The string array contains the *n* elements arg1 ... arg2. The string "java", optional command-line options, and the application class name do not appear in the array.

Exam Essentials

Know the contents of the argument list of an application's main method, given the command line that invoked the application. Be aware that the list is an array of Strings containing everything on the command line except the java command, command line options, and the name of the class.

Key Terms and Concepts

Application A Java class that contains a `public static void main(String[])` method, which can be invoked from the command line.

Argument list The command-line arguments passed into an application's main method.

Sample Questions

1. A user runs an application by typing "**java -verbosegc Wxyz 123.456 -remote**". How many items are in the argument list that is passed into the application's main method? (The "-verbosegc" option causes the Java virtual machine to print garbage collection information.)

    A. 2

    B. 3

    C. 4

    D. 5

    Answer: 2. The argument list contains only those strings that follow the application class name. Command-line options to the java command are not included.

2. Which of the following keywords must modify an application's main method?

A. final

B. int

C. private

D. protected

E. public

F. static

G. String[]

H. void

Answer: E, F, H. The main method must be public, static, and void.

Identify all Java programming language keywords and correctly constructed identifiers.

This objective is extremely fundamental. To create a name for a Java entity, you need to know the rules for name creation.

Critical Information

An identifier is the name of a class, interface, method, variable, or label. An identifier must begin with a letter, a dollar sign ($), or an underscore (_). Subsequent characters may be letters, dollar signs, underscores, or digits. Identifiers are case sensitive.

Certain strings that follow the above rule may not be used as identifiers because they are used by the Java language. These keywords are listed in Table 4.1.

TABLE 4.1: Java Keywords

abstract	do	implements	protected	throws
boolean	double	import	public	transient
break	else	instanceof	return	true
byte	extends	int	short	try
case	false	interface	static	void
catch	final	long	strictfp	volatile
char	finally	native	super	while
class	float	new	switch	
const	for	null	synchronized	
continue	goto	package	this	
default	if	private	throw	

Technically, true, false, and null are not keywords but predefined literals; however, the difference is slight and the exam is unlikely to test you on this detail. The words goto and const have no meaning in Java and may not be used as identifiers.

Exam Essentials

Distinguish between legal and illegal identifiers.   You should know the rules that restrict the first character and the subsequent characters of an identifier.

Recognize Java keywords.   You should recognize the keywords listed in Table 4.1.

Key Term and Concept

Identifier   The name of a class, interface, method, variable, or label.

Sample Questions

1. Which of the following are valid Java identifiers?

   A. $

   B. _$_

   C. $3.14159

   D. _3.14159

   Answer: A, B. Periods are not allowed in identifiers.

2. Which of the following are valid Java identifiers?

   A. abcde$

   B. switch

   C. GOTO

   D. label

   Answer: A, C, D. A, C, and D obey the rule for correctly constructed identifiers (C being legal because identifiers are case sensitive). B is illegal because it is a keyword.

State the effect of using a variable or array element of any kind when no explicit assignment has been made to it.

Java sometimes automatically initializes data, and sometimes it does not. It is important to know what data gets initialized under what circumstances, especially since the Java compiler is intolerant of uninitialized data. This objective tests your knowledge of data initialization.

Critical Information

Java supports variables of two different lifetimes:

- A member variable of a class is defined within the scope of the class and is accessible from any method in the class.

- An automatic variable of a method is defined within a method. An automatic variable is created on entry to the method, exists only during execution of the method, and is only accessible within the method.

Every member variable that is not explicitly assigned a value in its declaration is automatically assigned an initial value. The initialization value depends on the variable type, as shown in Table 4.2. Note that static variables are a kind of member variable, so they are automatically initialized.

When an array is constructed, all of its elements are initialized. Again, the initialization value depends on the variable type, as shown in Table 4.2.

The initialization values are zero for all numeric types. The literal notations that appear in the second column of the table are reviewed in the next objective.

TABLE 4.2: Initialization Values

Variable Type	Initial Value
byte	0
short	0
int	0
long	0L
float	0.0f
double	0.0d
boolean	false
char	'\u0000'
Object Reference	null

Exam Essentials

Know when Java initializes variables.   Initialization takes place when a class is constructed.

Know the initialization values for all data types.   Initialization types are given in Table 4.2.

Know that Java always initializes array elements.   Array elements are initialized to the same values as variables in classes.

Key Terms and Concepts

Automatic variable   A variable defined within the scope of a method.

Member variable   A variable defined within the scope of a class.

Sample Questions

1. In the class listed below, which variables are automatically initialized to zero?

```
class Q1 {
    int a;
    int b = 5;
    static int c;
    void aMethod() {
        int d;
    }
}
```

A. a

B. b

C. c

D. d

Answer: A, C. The variables a and c are automatically initialized because they are member variables that are not explicitly initialized. (c is considered a member variable even though it is static.) b is explicitly initialized to 5, so it does not need to be automatically initialized to zero. d is not a member variable, so it is not initialized.

2. In the code listed below, are the elements of array intarr automatically initialized to zero?

```
class Q2 {
void aMethod() {
    int[] intarr;
    intarr = new int[5];
  }
}
```

A. Yes

B. No

Answer: A. All arrays get their elements automatically initialized to zero at construction time, independent of the scope of the reference to the array.

State the range of all primitive data types and declare literal values for *String* and all primitive types using all permitted formats, bases, and representations.

This objective addresses the values that may legally be assigned to Java primitives. If you want to assign a literal value to a primitive, you must of course know the rules that govern literals. Moreover, any value that you assign to a primitive should fall within the range of the primitive. This objective tests your knowledge concerning assigning values to primitives.

Critical Information

This objective encompasses several concepts, which will be reviewed in turn:

- Primitive ranges
- Literal string values
- Literal character values
- Literal integral values
- Literal floating-point values

Primitive Ranges

Table 4.3 summarizes the value ranges for Java's four primitive integral data types.

TABLE 4.3: Integral Primitive Ranges

Type	Minimum Value	Maximum Value
byte	-2^7	2^7-1
short	-2^{15}	$2^{15}-1$
int	-2^{31}	$2^{31}-1$
long	-2^{63}	$2^{63}-1$

The general formula for the range of an n-bit integral primitive type is as follows:

- Minimum value = -2^n-1
- Minimum value = $2^{n-1}-1$

The char type is unsigned; it cannot take a negative value. The range of char is $0-2^{16}$.

The range of float is approximately $-3.4 * 10^{38} - +3.4 * 10^{38}$. The range of double is approximately $-1.8 * 10^{308} - +3.4 * 10^{308}$.

The boolean type cannot be strictly said to have a range. Its two possible values are true and false.

Literal Character and String Values

A char literal can be expressed by enclosing the desired character in single quotes, as shown here:

```
char c1 = 'k';
```

This technique only works if the desired character is available on the keyboard. Another way to express a char literal is as four hex digits, preceded by \u, with the expression enclosed in single quotes as shown below:

```
char cw = '\u13dd';    // Cherokee TLA
```

The u character has to be lowercase. Any non-digit hex characters may be lower- or uppercase.

Several additional char escape sequences are supported, as shown in Table 4.4.

TABLE 4.4:   Character Escape Sequence

Escape Sequence	Meaning
'\b'	Backspace
'\f'	Formfeed
'\n'	Newline
'\r'	Return
'\t'	Tab
'\''	Single quote
'\"'	Double quote
'\\'	Backslash

A string literal is a run of text enclosed in double quotes. The run may contain any of the escape sequences presented in this section.

Literal Integral Values

Integral literal values may be expressed in any of three bases:

- Decimal (the default)
- Octal
- Hexadecimal

The default base is decimal. To indicate octal, prefix the literal with 0 (zero). To indicate hexadecimal, prefix the literal with 0x or 0X. The characters a through f are hex digits that represent 10 through 15; they may be uppercase or lowercase. For example, the following three strings are equivalent ways to represent the value *twenty-eight*:

- 28
- 034
- 0x1c

Literal Floating-Point Values

A floating-point literal contains one of the following:

- A decimal point, e.g., 3.14159
- The letter e or E to indicate scientific notation, e.g., 1.23e + 41
- The suffix f or F to indicate a 32-bit float literal, e.g., −12.3f
- The suffix d or D to indicate a 64-bit double literal, e.g., −12.33333333333d

A floating-point literal with no f, F, d, or D suffix defaults to a 64-bit double literal.

Exam Essentials

State the ranges for each of Java's primitives.   Primitive ranges are listed in Table 4.3.

Recognize correctly formatted literals.   You should be familiar with all formats for literal characters, strings, and numbers.

Key Terms and Concepts

Floating-point literal   A floating-point literal either contains a decimal point, is expressed in scientific notation, or has the suffix f, F, d, or D.

Hexadecimal literal   A hex literal begins with 0x or 0X.

Octal literal   An octal literal begins with 0.

Sample Questions

1. Which of the following Java primitive types can express negative numbers?

A. boolean

B. byte

C. char

D. float

E. long

Answer: B, C, D. The boolean type is not numeric. The char type can only take zero and positive values.

2. Which of the following are valid literal Java strings?

A. "\"\""

B. "0xzabc"

C. '\'\''

D. "\t\t\r\n'

E. "boolean"

Answer: A, B, E. Strings C and D are not enclosed in double quotes.

3. Which of the following are valid literal Java numeric values?

A. 0xabcdeFg

B. 1.23e4

C. 3f

D. 3d

Answer: B, C, D. A is not valid because g is not a valid hex digit.

Chapter

5

Operators and Assignments

SUN CERTIFIED PROGRAMMER FOR JAVA 2 PLATFORM EXAM OBJECTIVES COVERED IN THIS CHAPTER:

- Determine the result of applying any operator, including assignment operators, *instanceof,* and casts, to operands of any type class, scope or accessibility, or any combination of these.

- Determine the result of applying *boolean equals(Object)* method to objects of any combination of the classes *java.lang.String, java.lang.Boolean,* and *java.lang.Object.*

- In an expression involving the operators &, |, &&, ||, and variables of known values, state which operands are evaluated and the value of the expression.

- Determine the effect upon objects and primitive values of passing variables into methods and performing assignments or other modifying operations in that method.

The whole point of computers is to process data; that's what they're for. Operators do the processing. Java's operators can surprise you: Their behavior can be unexpected and sometimes unwelcome, as you no doubt saw the first time you tried to add two bytes together and assign the result to a byte.

The objectives covered in this chapter make sure you have a thorough understanding of Java's operators.

Determine the result of applying any operator, including assignment operators, *instanceof*, and casts, to operands of any type class, scope or accessibility, or any combination of these.

This objective ensures that you are completely familiar with the functionality of every Java operator in every context. This familiarity is vital, because writing code that produces unexpected results is always disastrous.

Critical Information

Java's operators can be grouped into nine categories, which are listed below in approximate descending order of execution precedence.

- Unary operators: ++ -- + - ! ~

- The cast operator: ()

- Binary arithmetic operators: * / % + -

- Shift operators: << >> >>>

- Comparison operators: < <= > >= == != instanceof

- Bitwise operators: & ^ |

- Short-circuit operators: && ||

- The ternary operator: ?:

- Assignment operators: = op=

Before examining each of these categories, we will review arithmetic promotion, which affects all unary and binary arithmetic operators.

Arithmetic Promotion

The result of a unary or binary arithmetic operation does not always have the same type as the operand or operands. The JVM performs *arithmetic promotion*, the conversion of an arithmetic operand to a wider type. Primitive type A is wider than primitive type B if the range of A completely encompasses the range of B. Figure 5.1 shows the width relationships among Java's numeric primitives. In the figure, any type A is wider than any other type B if you can get from type A to type B by following the arrows.

Remember that in this context, width refers to the range of a type, rather than number of bits.

FIGURE 5.1: Relative widths of primitive types

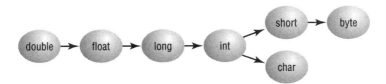

The result of any Java arithmetic is always of type `int` or wider. For unary arithmetic, if the single operand is of type `byte`, `short`, or `char`, it is promoted to an `int` of equal value; the operation is applied to the `int`, and the result is of type `int`. No promotion takes place during unary arithmetic on an `int`, `long`, `float`, or `double`.

For binary arithmetic, conversion follows these two steps:

- If either operand is a `byte`, `short`, or `char`, it is promoted to an `int`.

- If the operands are now of different types, the narrower operand is promoted to the type of the wider operand. The result of the operation has the same type as the operands.

Table 5.1 shows the result types of all possible combinations of binary arithmetic operand types.

TABLE 5.1:   Binary Arithmetic Result Types

	byte	short	char	int	long	float	double
byte	int	int	int	int	long	float	double
short	int	int	int	int	long	float	double
char	int	int	int	int	long	float	double
int	int	int	int	int	long	float	double
long	long	long	long	long	long	float	double
float	float	float	float	float	float	float	double
double	double	double	double	double	double	double	double

Unary Operators: *++ -- + - ! ~*

The increment and decrement operators ++ and -- can be applied to any primitive type except `boolean`. The operators add or subtract 1 from their operands. Both operators can appear in prefix or postfix form. The difference is significant when the operation appears within an expression. The prefix form (for example, ++x or --y) performs the operation before the expression is evaluated; the postfix form (for example, x++ or y--) performs the operation after the expression is evaluated.

The following code fragment illustrates the prefixed increment operator.

```
1. int x = 8;
2. int y = ++x * 10;
```

After line 2 executes, the value of x is 9. The value of y is 90, because x is incremented before evaluation of the expression ++x * 10.

In the following code, the increment operator is postfixed.

```
1. int x = 8;
2. int y = x++ * 10;
```

After line 2 executes, the value of x is again 9. However, now the value of y is 80, because x is incremented after evaluation of the expression x++ * 10.

The sign operators + and - can be applied to any primitive type except boolean. As a unary operator, + is purely cosmetic: it maintains the sign of its operand. The - operator reverses the sign of its operand.

The boolean complement operator ! (often pronounced "bang") can only be applied to operands of type boolean. The operator inverts the truth value of its operand; thus !true is false, and !false is true.

The bitwise inversion operator ~ can only be applied to operands of integral numerical type: byte, short, int, long, and char. The operator inverts all the bits of the operand. If the operator is applied to one of the signed numeric types (byte, short, int, long), then the sign bit is inverted along with all the magnitude bits.

Table 5.2 summarizes which unary operators can be applied to which primitive data types.

TABLE 5.2: Unary Operator Application

Operator	Operand Type							
	boolean	byte	short	char	int	long	float	double
++, --	No	✓	✓	✓	✓	✓	✓	✓
+, -	No	✓	✓	✓	✓	✓	✓	✓
!	✓	No	No	No	No	No	No	No
~	No	✓	✓	✓	✓	✓	No	No

The Cast Operator: ()

The cast operator can be applied to any primitive or reference. The result is a primitive or reference of a new type. The new type appears between the parentheses, which prefix the operand. For example, suppose class Grapefruit extends class Citrus. If c is a reference variable of type Citrus, then (Grapefruit)c is a reference of type Grapefruit; both references point to the same object.

There are many rules that govern which types may be cast to which other types. There are two large-scale rules:

- You can't cast from a primitive to a reference, or vice versa.

- You can't cast from or to a boolean.

Primitive casting is easy: any non-boolean type can be cast to any other non-boolean type. However, if the new type is wider than the old type, the cast is not required. (Refer to Figure 5.1 to see the relative widths of Java's primitive types.) The following code fragment is an example of primitive casting.

```
1. int z = 50;
2. byte b = (byte)z;
```

The cast in line 2 is required because int is wider than byte. Whenever the old type is wider than the new type (that is, whenever the cast is necessary), there is a danger at runtime of data loss. When both the old and new types are integral, the cast operates by writing as many low-order bits from the old value as will fit to the new value; any high-order bits that do not fit are discarded. In the previous example, the new value consists of the low-order 8 bits of the old value; the high-order 24 bits are discarded. The largest positive byte value is 127. If z in line 1 were, for example, 129, there would be a problem. The new value would be 1. When a cast results in data loss, no exception is thrown.

Object reference casting is governed by a large number of rules. The two most important rules are as follows:

- When the old and new types are both classes, one class must be a superclass of the other class. However, if the new type is a superclass of the old type, then the cast is not required.

- When one type is an interface and the other type is a class, then the class must implement the interface. However, if the new type is an interface, then the cast is not required.

The following code illustrates object reference casting. Assume class Child extends class Parent, which implements interface Inter.

```
1. Child  c1 = new Child();
2. Parent p1 = (Parent)c1;   // Cast not required
3. Child  c2 = (Child)p1;    // Cast required
4. Inter  i1 = (Inter)p1;    // Cast not required
5. Parent p2 = (Parent)i1;   // Cast required
```

When you cast object references, there is a runtime danger that the new type will be incompatible with the object being referenced, even though the compile-time rules are obeyed. For example, consider the following code:

```
1. String s = new String("abc");
2. Object ob = s;           // Cast not required
3. Thread t = (Thread)ob;   // Compiles but throws
```

This code throws ClassCastException at line 3.

Binary Arithmetic Operators: * / % + -

Java's binary arithmetic operators are fairly straightforward. Remember that arithmetic promotion is always at work. All five operators are allowed to operate on any combination of numeric types.

No matter what the result of the operation is, there are only two ways to generate an exception:

- Dividing an integral type (byte, short, int, or long) by integer zero.

- Taking an integral type modulo integer zero.

Both of these operations throw ArithmeticException.

Overflow does not generate an exception. If the result of an arithmetic operation requires more bits than the result type has, the overflow high-end bits are discarded.

Shift Operators: << >> >>>

The three Java shift operators perform left shift (<<), signed right shift (>>), and unsigned right shift (>>>). These operators operate on integral primitive types. Due to arithmetic promotion, the result will always be an int or a long.

The left shift operation (<<) shifts zeros into the low-order end of the result and discards bits from the high-order end, as shown in Figure 5.2. Performing a left shift by n bits is equivalent to multiplying by 2^n.

The unsigned right shift operation (>>>) shifts zeros into the high-order end of the result and discards bits from the low-order end, as shown in Figure 5.3.

FIGURE 5.2: Left shift

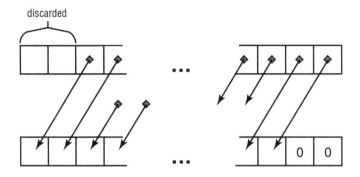

FIGURE 5.3: Unsigned right shift

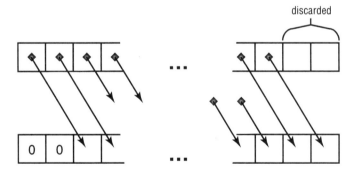

The signed right shift operation (>>) extends the sign bit into the high-order end of the result and discards bits from the low-order end, as shown in Figure 5.4. Performing a signed right shift by n bits is equivalent to dividing by 2^n.

FIGURE 5.4: Signed right shift

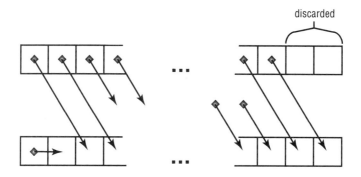

Comparison Operators: < <= > >= == != *instanceof*

The comparison operators all return a boolean value. They can take various types of operand, as shown in Table 5.3. (The instanceof keyword is commonly considered a comparison operator because it returns a boolean, so it is included in this section.)

TABLE 5.3: Operands of the Comparison Operators

Operator	Type of 1st Operand	Type of 2nd Operand
<	Any primitive except boolean	Any primitive except boolean
<=	Any primitive except boolean	Any primitive except boolean
>	Any primitive except boolean	Any primitive except boolean
>=	Any primitive except boolean	Any primitive except boolean
==	Any primitive or reference	Any primitive or reference
!=	Any primitive or reference	Any primitive or reference
instanceof	Reference	Class or interface name

The <, <=, >, and >= operators are straightforward. The == and != operators are straightforward when the operands are primitives. When the operands are references, the operators test for *reference equality*. This means that the references are checked to see if they point to the same object. (This is distinct from *object equality*, under which two different objects are considered equal if their significant instance variables are equal. The next objective concerns object equality.)

The format of the `instanceof` operator is

```
<reference> instanceof <class_or_interface_name>
```

The first operand is an object reference. The second operand is the name of a class or interface. The operation considers the class of the object pointed to by the reference. (This is distinct from the type of reference; the class of the object can only be known at runtime.) If the second operand is a class name, the operator returns `true` if the class of the object the first operand points to is the same class as, or a subclass of, the class name. If the second operand is an interface name, the operator returns `true` if the class of the object the first operand points to implements the interface.

Bitwise Operators: *& ^ |*

The bitwise operators act on two booleans or on two integral numeric operands. In the latter case, arithmetic promotion ensures that the two operands are the same type. Bitwise operation on integral numeric operands works on all bit positions of the operands, including the sign bit. The & operator performs the logical "and" function; the ^ operator performs the logical "exclusive or" function; the | operator performs the logical "or" function.

Short-Circuit Operators: *&& ||*

The operators && and || perform *short-circuit* operations. A short-circuit operation does not evaluate its second operand if evaluation of the first operand determines the result of the operation. Thus && performs a logical "and" on the operands and only evaluates its second operand if the first operand is `true`; if the first operand is `false`, there is no need to evaluate the second operand. Similarly, || performs a logical "or" and only evaluates its second operand if the first operand is false. Note that there is no short-circuit "xor" operand.

The following method illustrates the short-circuit && operator.

```
1. char getSecondChar(String s) {
2.   if (s != null && s.length() >= 2)
3.     return s.charAt(2);
4.   return '?';
5. }
```

If the method is called with a null argument, then the first operand of && on line 2 evaluates to false, so evaluation of the second operand is short-circuited. This is fortunate, since evaluating the second operand with s equal to null would result in a NullPointerException.

The Ternary Operator: *? :*

The ternary operator is shorthand for coding simple conditions into a single expression. The ternary operator has the following format:

```
<boolean_expression> ? <expressionA> :
<expressionB>
```

The boolean expression is evaluated first. If its value is true, the result of the ternary operator is expression A; otherwise the result of the ternary operator is expression B.

Assignment Operators: *= op=*

The equals sign (=) is an operator; it returns a value as illustrated below:

```
1. int a, b;
2. a = (b=5) * 100;
```

The value of the assignment operator is the value that is assigned to the left-hand variable, so in line 2 the value of (b=5) is 5. After line 2 executes, b is 5 and a is 500.

The "calculate and assign" operators are often denoted as "op=" operators. These operators consist of any of the binary non-boolean operators, followed by the equals sign (=). In general, the expression "x op= y" is shorthand for "x = x op y". For example, "x /= y" is shorthand for "x = x / y". Be aware that side effects in the expression x are only evaluated once, not twice as the expanded view might suggest.

If the value being assigned has a different type from the left-hand side of the assignment, there are two possible outcomes:

- If the types are compatible, the data type will be converted.

- If the types are incompatible, the compiler will generate an error. The error says that an explicit cast is required.

The important point here is type compatibility. For primitives, the new type must be the same as, or wider than, the old type. (Wider types are discussed at the beginning of this chapter, in the "Arithmetic Promotion" section. For a quick review, see Figure 5.1.) For references, there is a bewildering number of combinations of possibilities, but the main rules are the following:

- If both old and new types are classes, the new type must be the same as, or a superclass of, the new type.

- If the new type is an interface, the old type must implement that interface.

- In the new type is Object, the old type may be almost anything, including an array.

The following code illustrates several legal assignment conversions.

```
1. int i = 15;
2. float f = i;            // int to float
3.
4. Button btn = new Button("OK");
5. Component c = btn;       // class to superclass
6.
7. FlowLayout fl = new FlowLayout();
```

```
8. LayoutManager lm = fl; // class to interface
9.
10. double[] dubs = new double[33];
11. Object ob = dubs;      // array to Object
```

Line 2 converts an `int` to a `float`. Line 5 converts a class to a superclass (`java.awt.Button` extends `java.awt.Component`). Line 8 converts a class to an interface implemented by the class (class `java.awt.FlowLayout` implements interface `java.awt.LayoutManager`). Line 11 converts an array to an `Object`.

Exam Essentials

Understand when arithmetic promotion takes place. You should know the type of the result of unary and binary arithmetic operations performed on operands of any type.

Understand the functionality of all the operators discussed in this section. These operators are

Unary operators: ++ -- + - ! ~

The cast operator: ()

Binary arithmetic operators: * / % + -

Shift operators: << >> >>>

Comparison operators: < <= > >= == != instanceof

Bitwise operators: & ^ |

Short-circuit operators: && ||

The ternary operator: ?:

Assignment operators: = op=

Know that assignment promotion takes place when the new type is wider than the old type. You need to be familiar with the width relationships among Java's numeric primitive types, as depicted in Figure 5.1.

Key Terms and Concepts

Arithmetic exception   This exception type is only thrown on integer divide by zero or integer modulo zero.

Arithmetic promotion   Conversion of an arithmetic operand to a wider type.

Assignment promotion   Conversion during assignment of a primitive or object reference to a compatible type.

Reference equality   Tests for whether two references point to the same object.

Short-circuit operation   A short-circuit operation does not evaluate its second operand if evaluation of the first operand determines the result of the operation.

Signed right shift   A shift where the magnitude bits are shifted and the sign bit is extended.

Unsigned shift   A shift where all bits are shifted.

Wider type   Primitive type A is wider than primitive type B if the range of A completely encompasses the range of B.

Sample Questions

1. When you divide a `byte` by a no-zero `char`, what is the type of the result?

  A. `byte`

  B. `char`

  C. `int`

  D. `float`

  E. `double`

  Answer: C. The operands are both promoted to `int`, and the result is an `int`.

2. Which of the following code fragments generate an exception?

A. `int x = 10; int y = 0; int z = x/y;`

B. `float x = 10f; float y = 0f; float z = x/y;`

C. `int x = 10; int y = 0; int z = x%y;`

Answer: A and C. The only ways to generate an exception from an arithmetic operation are to divide or modulo an integer by integer zero.

3. Which of the following code fragments is equivalent to dividing x by 8?

A. `x << 3`

B. `x << 8`

C. `x >> 3`

D. `x >> 3`

E. `x >>> 8`

F. `x >>> 3`

Answer: D. The signed right shift (>>) divides by 2^n.

4. Which of the following are Java short-circuit operators?

A. `&`

B. `&&`

C. `|`

D. `||`

E. `^`

F. `^^`

Answer: B, D. The && and || operators short-circuit evaluation of their second operand. There is no ^^ operator in Java.

5. Does the following code fragment compile?

```
1. byte b = 8;
2. char c = b;
```

A. Yes

B. No

Answer: B. The code does not compile because the char type is not wider than the byte type.

Determine the result of applying *boolean equals(Object)* method to objects of any combination of the classes *java.lang.String, java.lang.Boolean,* and *java.lang.Object.*

This objective looks at the equals() method, which is used in Java for determining object equality. Object equality is important in its own right; moreover, the Collections API relies heavily on the equals() method. (The Collections API is discussed in Chapter 10, "The *java.util* Package.") This objective recognizes the importance of the equals() method and object equality.

Critical Information

Object equality tests whether two possibly distinct objects are identical in the values of their important instance variables. Object equality is different from the more rigorous reference equality (discussed earlier in this chapter), which tests whether two references point to the same object. Under object equality, two different objects are considered equal if they resemble each other closely enough.

Object equality is tested by calling the equals() method, which all classes inherit from the java.lang.Object superclass. The objective requires you to be familiar with the functionality of the equals() method of the Object, Boolean, and String classes. The equals() method has the following signature:

```
public boolean equals(Object ob)
```

The equals() method of the Object class returns true if the current object is the same object as the ob argument. In other words, this version of the method simply tests for reference equality. The equals() method of the Boolean class returns true if the ob argument is an instance of Boolean and encapsulates the same value as the current object. The equals() method of the String class returns true if the ob argument is an instance of String and encapsulates a string that is identical to the one encapsulated by the current object.

Table 5.4 summarizes the result of calling equals() on and with all possible combinations of the Object, Boolean, and String classes. The columns denote the true class of the argument, not the type of the reference; this is in keeping with the wording of the objective.

TABLE 5.4: Calling equals() on Object, Boolean, and String

Class of Current Object	Class of Argument		
	Object	Boolean	String
Object	Revert to ==	Revert to ==	Revert to ==
Boolean	if (ob instanceof Boolean), compare encapsulated value, else return false	Compare encapsulated value	false
String	if (ob instanceof String), compare encapsulated string, else return false	false	Compare encapsulated string

Exam Essentials

Understand the difference between object equality and reference equality. Object equality checks the data of two possibly distinct objects. Reference equality checks whether two references point to the same object.

Know the functionality of the **equals()** method of the **Object,
Boolean,** and **String** classes.   The Object version reverts to a reference equality check; the Boolean and String versions compare encapsulated data.

Key Term and Concept

Object equality   A test for whether two possibly distinct objects are identical in the values of their important instance variables.

Sample Questions

1. In the code fragment below, does line 4 execute?

```
1. Boolean boo = new Boolean(true);
2. Object ob = new Boolean(true);
3. if (ob.equals(boo))
4.    System.out.println("Hello world.");
```

A. Yes

B. No

Answer: A. The type of reference ob is Object, but the class of what ob points to is Boolean. Thus it is the equals() method of class Boolean that gets called.

2. In the code fragment below, does line 4 execute?

```
1. Object o1 = new Object();
2. Object o2 = new Object();
3. if (o1.equals(o2))
4.    System.out.println("Hello world.");
```

A. Yes

B. No

Answer: B. The equals() method of Object class is just a test for reference equality. Since two distinct objects are being compared, the equals() method returns false.

In an expression involving the operators &, |, &&, ||, and variables of known values, state which operands are evaluated and the value of the expression.

This objective focuses on the difference between the short-circuit operators && and || and the ordinary operators & and |. These operators were already reviewed in the first objective of this chapter, so we will not discuss them further.

Determine the effect upon objects and primitive values of passing variables into methods and performing assignments or other modifying operations in that method.

This objective addresses Java's argument-passing structure. Some languages pass by reference and some pass by value. The terminology is unimportant, but understanding the functionality is vital. If you don't understand how arguments are passed, you could be surprised when data changes or disappointed when it doesn't. Either way, your code will not operate as expected.

Critical Information

Java passes primitives and object references by value. This means that when data is passed into the method, the method receives a copy of the original data. No matter what changes the method makes to its copy, the original value is not affected.

Passing by value is easy to understand in the case of primitive data. Consider the following method and code fragment:

```
1. void halfOf(int i) { i /= 2; }
 . . .
2. int z = 20;
3. halfOf(z);
```

After line 3, z is still 20. When halfOf() is called, a copy of z is created and passed into the method. The copy is divided by two, but the original is unaffected.

The situation is more complicated when the method argument is an object reference. As Java programmers, we never directly handle objects; we use references, which are returned by constructors. When a reference is passed into a method call, the method receives a copy of the reference. Of course, the copy points to the same object as the original reference. If the method uses the reference to modify the object, the modifications are permanent. However, if the method changes the value of the reference itself, such changes do not affect the original reference.

Exam Essentials

Understand that primitive and reference method arguments are passed by value.   Method arguments are not permanently affected by modifications within the method.

Key Term and Concept

Passing by value   Method arguments are copies of the values passed into the method; changes made within the method do not affect the original values.

Sample Questions

1. What value is printed out on line 8 when the following application is run?

```
1. class Bumper {
2.    double d=10;
3.    void bump(Bumper b) { b.d++; }
4.
5.    public static void main(String[] args) {
6.       Bumper myBumper = new Bumper();
7.       myBumper.bump(myBumper);
8.       System.out.println(myBumper.d);
9.    }
10. }
```

A. 10

B. 11

Answer: B. The method on line 3 receives a reference to a Bumper. Modifications of b within the method have no effect on the original value (myBumper in the main method). However, modifications to the object pointed to by b are permanent.

2. What value is printed out on line 9 when the following application is run?

```
1. class Halfer {
2.    static void split(int z) {
3.       z /= 2;
4.    }
5.
6.    public static void main(String[] args) {
7.       int splitme = 10;
8.       split(splitme);
9.       System.out.println(splitme);
10.   }
11. }
```

A. 10

B. 5

Answer: A. The method on line 2 receives a copy of its argument and splits the copy, leaving the original value intact.

Chapter

6

Overloading, Overriding, Runtime Type, and Object Orientation

SUN CERTIFIED PROGRAMMER FOR JAVA 2 PLATFORM EXAM OBJECTIVES COVERED IN THIS CHAPTER:

State the benefits of encapsulation in object-oriented design and write code that implements tightly encapsulated classes and the relationships "is a" and "has a".

Write code to invoke overridden or overloaded methods and parental or overloaded constructors; and describe the effect of invoking these methods.

Write code to construct instances of any concrete class including normal top level classes, inner classes, static inner classes, and anonymous inner classes.

he objectives in this group are all concerned with how Java implements features that are common to most object-oriented programming languages. These features include encapsulation, polymorphism, classes, and subclasses. Knowing how to deal with these features is essential for writing good object-oriented code in any language. These objectives make sure your object-oriented foundation in Java is strong.

State the benefits of encapsulation in object-oriented design and write code that implements tightly encapsulated classes and the relationships "is a" and "has a".

This objective is about encapsulation, which is one of the fundamental five-syllable concepts of object-oriented programming. The "is a" and "has a" relationships are important because object-oriented analysis and design often result in documents that emphasize these relationships. UML (Unified Modeling Language), which is the current de facto standard for drawing object-oriented systems, includes symbols for depicting the "is a" and "has a" relationships.

Critical Information

This objective covers three concepts:

- Encapsulation
- The "is a" relationship

- The "has a" relationship

We will review each of these concepts in turn.

Encapsulation

Encapsulation provides many important benefits. Probably most important is that it makes object-oriented programming possible. Another major benefit is maintainability. Good encapsulation means that a class is completely responsible for the internal representation of data; thus, no other classes need to worry about how the class represents data. This principle is illustrated as follows:

```
import java.awt.Color;
class Car {
    private Color myColor;
    public void setColor(Color c) { myColor = c; }
    public Color getColor()        { return myColor; }
}
```

Here the internal representation of the car's color is an instance of java.awt.Color. In keeping with good encapsulation principles, other classes cannot directly read or modify the color; they must call the *accessor* and *mutator* methods setColor() and getColor(). An accessor is a public method that returns private data; a mutator is a public method that modifies private data. If the internal representation of a car's color changes (for example, to red/green/blue ints, to hue/saturation/brightness ints, to a paint product part number, or to a color name string), the accessor and mutator methods will have to be modified. However, classes that use the color (by calling the accessor and mutator) will continue to function correctly.

The "Is A" Relationship

The "is a" relationship is a human-language way of saying that one class extends another class. For example, an object-oriented analysis might state that a dog is a mammal and a golden retriever is a dog. Here the phrase "is a ..." can be taken to mean "is a kind of ...". The analysis would result in three classes: Mammal, Dog, and GoldenRetriever, where Dog extends Mammal, and GoldenRetriever extends Dog.

Be aware that there are times when the phrase "is a" occurs in object-oriented analysis or common speech, when it does *not* imply class extension. For example, someone might say "Harley is a golden retriever," meaning that "Harley" is the name of an individual golden retriever. In the domain on object-oriented programming, Harley would be an instance rather than a class.

The "Has A" Relationship

The "has a" relationship is a human-language way of saying that a class contains a member variable. For example, an object-oriented analysis might state that an employee has a salary, a hire date, and a manager. In the domain of code, the corresponding Employee class might have members called salary, hireDate, and manager. The following code is one reasonable implementation of the Employee class.

```
public class Employee {
    private float    salary;
    private Data     hireDate;
    private Employee manager;
    . . .
}
```

Note that the three member variables are private. Presumably, other classes will use them via the public accessor and mutator methods.

Exam Essentials

Be familiar with the way the Java language realizes the "is a" and "has a" relationships. The "is a" relationship implies class extension. The "has a" relationship implies ownership of a reference to a different object.

Key Terms and Concepts

Accessor   A public method that returns private data.

"Has a"   "X has a Y" means that class X owns a variable of type Y.

"Is a"   "X is a Y" means that class X extends class Y.

Mutator   A public method that modifies private data.

Sample Questions

1. Which of the following is the best approach to encapsulation?

   A. Private data, private accessors and mutators.

   B. Private data, public accessors and mutators.

   C. Public data, private accessors and mutators.

   D. Public data, public accessors and mutators.

   Answer: B. Private data and public accessors/mutators provide the cleanest maintenance situation.

2. An object-oriented analysis produces the following sentence: "A duck is a bird that has a beak." When the analysis is converted into code, which of the following will be true?

   A. Class Duck extends class Bird.

   B. Class Bird extends class Duck.

   C. Class Beak extends class Duck.

   D. Class Duck extends class Beak.

   Answer: A. The "is a" relationship corresponds to class extension. The "has a" relationship does not concern extension.

Write code to invoke overridden or overloaded methods and parental or overloaded constructors; and describe the effect of invoking these methods.

This objective tests your understanding of overloading and overriding, and of invoking parental methods and constructors. Without this understanding, you will not be able to take full advantage of the methods you write.

Critical Information

This objective covers four related topics:

- Overriding
- Overloading
- Overloaded constructors
- Parental constructors

In the next four sections, we will review each of these topics in turn.

Overriding

Overriding is the reuse of a method name in a class hierarchy. For example, consider a class called Building that has a method called protected float washWindows(int z) and a subclass of Building called House. The House class inherits the washWindows() method. In the absence of any overriding, calling washWindows() on an instance of House results in execution of the method as it appears in the Building superclass.

The House class can *override* the inherited method by providing its own version, with exactly the same name, argument list, and return value as the superclass's version. (The compiler will generate an error if the name and argument list are the same and the return value is different. It is legal to have the same name and a different argument list, but this is not an example of overriding.)

Now consider the following code fragment:

```
1. Building bldg = new House();
2. bldg.washWindows();
```

When the washWindows() method is called in line 2, it is the House class's version that executes, not the Building class's version. This is because method version is determined by the runtime type of the object that is executing a method. *Runtime type* is the true class of an object, as opposed to the type of a reference that points to that object. In the example, bldg is a reference, of type Building, to an object whose class or runtime type is House. The runtime type is determined by what constructor was called when the object was created; runtime type never changes throughout the lifetime of an object, even though references of many different types may point to the object. In our example, we know that the object's runtime type is House, because the House constructor is called on line 1.

A method may not be overridden to become more private. Thus the following rules apply:

- A public method may only be overridden by a public method.

- A protected method may only be overridden by a public method or a protected method.

- A default method may only be overridden by a public method, a protected method, or a default method.

- A private method may be overridden by a method of any access mode.

You may sometimes want to invoke the superclass's version of a method that is overridden in the current class. This is achieved by using the super keyword as a reference. Thus, for example, code anywhere in the House class may call the washWindows() method of the Building superclass by invoking super.washWindows().

This use of super is not recursive; you may not invoke, for example, super.super.washWindows().

Overloading

Overloading is reuse of a method name within a class. Two methods with the same name must have different argument lists; the compiler generates an error if the names and argument lists are the same and only the return values are different. There are no restrictions on access modes for overloaded methods.

The following class contains an example of legal overloading:

```
1. class C1 {
2.   public int abc(float f, String s) { ... }
3.   protected void abc() { ... }
4. }
```

The following class does not compile; it contains illegal overloading.

```
1. class C2 {
2.   public int abc(float f, String s) { ... }
3.   public char abc(float f, String s) { ... }
4. }
```

The overloading in the class above is illegal because the two methods have the same name and argument lists, differing only in their return types.

Overloaded Constructors

Constructors, as well as methods, may be overloaded. Overloaded constructors must have different argument lists. Of course, name and return type are not issues, because a constructor's name is restricted to be the name of the class, and there is no return type.

The following code is an example of a class with three overloaded constructors.

```
1. class Xyz {
2.     int a;
3.     int b;
4.     int c;
5.
6.     Xyz() {
7.         a = 10;
8.         b = 20;
9.     }
10.
11.     Xyz(int n) {
12.         a = 10;
13.         b = 20;
14.         c = n;
15.     }
16.
17.     Xyz(String s) {
18.         a = 10;
19.         b = 20;
20.         System.out.println(s);
21.     }
22. }
```

In the example above, lines 12–13 and lines 18–19 just repeat the functionality of the constructor at lines 6–9. (Such a constructor, which takes no arguments, is known as a *default constructor.*) It would be more efficient (and more maintainable) if the constructors could invoke other constructors. This can be done with the this keyword, which here means something different from its usual meaning of "pointer to current object." Here, the this keyword must appear in the first line of a constructor and is followed by a parenthetical argument list. The types in the argument list must correspond to the types of one of the class's constructors, which gets invoked. The example above is rewritten as follows to use the new syntax.

```
1. class Xyz {
2.    int a;
3.    int b;
4.    int c;
5.
6.    Xyz() {      // Default constructor
7.       a = 10;
8.       b = 20;
9.    }
10.
11.   Xyz(int n) {
12.      this(); // Invoke default constructor
13.      c = n;
14.   }
15.
16.   Xyz(String s) {
17.      this;    // Invoke default constructor
18.      System.out.println(s);
19.   }
20. }
```

Lines 12 and 17 use the this keyword to invoke the constructor on lines 6–9.

Parental Constructors

Every constructor begins execution by invoking the constructor of the immediate superclass. (The superclass's constructor does the same, so the process is recursive up to the ultimate superclass, which is Object.) If you do not explicitly specify which superclass constructor you want invoked, the compiler generates code that automatically calls the superclass's default constructor. This situation is illustrated in the following code:

```
1. class Bird {
2.    Bird() {
3.       System.out.println("Bird dflt");
```

```
4.    }
5.  }
6.
7.  class Poultry extends Bird {
8.     Poultry() {
9.        System.out.println("Poultry dflt");
10.    }
11. }
12.
13. class Turkey extends Poultry {
14.    Turkey () {
15.       System.out.println("Turkey dflt");
16.    }
17.    Turkey (int x) {
18.       System.out.println("Turkey other");
19.    }
20. }
```

When either Turkey constructor is called, the first thing that happens is the invisible call to the Poultry default constructor, where the first thing that happens is the invisible call to the Bird default constructor (which invisibly calls the Object default constructor). For example, if the Turkey constructor on line 17 is called, the output will be as follows:

```
Bird dflt
Poultry dflt
Turkey other
```

If you don't want to invoke the default parent constructor, you can invoke a different constructor by using the super keyword, which must appear on the first line of a constructor. In the following code, the Poultry constructor has been overloaded, and the Turkey default constructor has been modified to call a non-default Poultry constructor.

```
1. class Bird {
2.    Bird() {
```

```
3.        System.out.println("Bird dflt");
4.   }
5. }
6.
7. class Poultry extends Bird {
8.    Poultry() {
9.        System.out.println("Poultry dflt");
10.   }
11.    Poultry(double d) {
12.        System.out.println("Poultry other");
13. }
14.
15. class Turkey extends Poultry {
16.    Turkey () {
17.        super(12.34);
18.        System.out.println("Turkey dflt");
19.   }
20.    Turkey (int x) {
21.        System.out.println("Turkey other");
22.   }
23. }
```

Now when the Turkey default constructor is called, the overloaded Poultry constructor on lines 11–13 is called, so the output is as follows:

```
Bird dflt
Poultry other
Turkey dflt
```

This recursive mechanism of calling superclass constructors depends on the existence of superclass constructors. The Java compiler guarantees the existence of a constructor for every class. If you create a class and do not explicitly provide it with any constructors, the compiler invisibly creates a default constructor. This free, invisible default constructor does nothing except invoke the default constructor of the superclass.

Exam Essentials

Be able to identify legally overridden methods. The methods must have the same name, argument list, and return type.

Be able to identify legally overloaded methods and constructors. The methods/constructors must have different argument lists.

Understand the chain of calls to parental constructors. Each constructor invocation begins by invoking a parental constructor.

Know how to create a constructor that invokes a non-default parental constructor. Understand the use of the super keyword.

Key Terms and Concepts

Default constructor A constructor that takes no arguments.

Overloading Reuse of a method name within a class.

Overriding Reuse of a method name in a subclass.

Runtime type Class of an object (versus type of a reference).

Sample Questions

1. Consider the following class definition:

```
class Zzz {
    int aaa(int j) { return 4; }
}
```

Which of the following methods, considered individually, would be legal in a subclass of Zzz?

A. byte aaa(int j) { ... }

B. long aaa(int j) { ... }

C. int aaa(int j) { ... }

D. `int aaa(boolean b) { ... }`

E. `void aaa(boolean b) { ... }`

Answer: C, D, and E. A and B are illegal because they change the return type of the superclass's version of the method, while retaining the name and the argument list. C is an example of legal overriding. D and E retain the name but not the argument list of the superclass's version, so they are not examples of overriding; thus, there are no restrictions on their return types, and they are legal.

2. Consider the following class definition:

```
class Zzz {
   int aaa(int j) { return 4; }
}
```

Which of the following methods, considered individually, would be legal in a subclass of Zzz?

A. `int aaa(int j) { ... }`

B. `private int aaa(int j) { ... }`

C. `protected int aaa(int j) { ... }`

D. `public int aaa(int j) { ... }`

Answer: A, C, D. A method may not be overridden to be more private. The method in the Zzz superclass has default access, so the overriding version in the subclass may have default, protected, or public access. Private access is not allowed.

3. Consider the following class definition:

```
class Zzz {
   int aaa(int j) { return 4; }
}
```

Which of the following methods, considered individually, would be legal in class Zzz?

A. `int aaa(float j) { ... }`

B. `float aaa(int j) { ... }`

C. `int aaa(int j, String s) { ... }`

D. `float aaa(int j, Character c) { ... }`

Answer: A, C, D. An overloading method has the same name as the method being overloaded and must have a different argument list. When deciding whether a method is legally overriding, do not consider return type.

4. Consider the following class definition:

```
class Yyy {
    double a, b;
    Yyy(int i, int j) {
        a = Math.sqrt(i*i*i - j*j+365);
        b = Math.random() + a;
        a /= b;
    }
}
```

You wish to add another constructor to class Yyy. The new constructor will take no arguments and should perform exactly as the constructor listed above were called with i=0 and j=1. Which of the following constructors delivers the desired behavior?

A. `Yyy() { Yyy(0, 1); }`

B. `Yyy() { this(0, 1); }`

C. `Yyy() { super(0, 1); }`

Answer: B. The keyword this invokes an overloaded constructor of the current class.

Write code to construct instances of any concrete class including normal top level classes, inner classes, static inner classes, and anonymous inner classes.

Inner classes are an extremely important feature of the Java language. When used wisely, they can greatly contribute to the maintainability of a program. However, inner classes are fraught with subtleties. The exam requires you to be familiar with all the ins and outs of inner classes.

Critical Information

An *inner class* is a class that is defined within another class, known as the *enclosing class*. There are four kinds of inner class:

- Simple inner classes
- Inner classes in methods
- Anonymous inner classes
- Static inner classes

Each of these species reveals new, subtle, and sometimes bizarre behavior. We will examine each one in turn. We will then examine use of inner classes from within static code.

Simple Inner Classes

The simplest kind of inner class is defined within its enclosing class, on the same level as the methods and data of the enclosing class. The inner class has access to all the data and methods of the enclosing class (even the private data and methods), as shown below.

```
1. class Outer extends java.util.Vector {
2.    int x, y;
3.    private int z;
```

```
 4.
 5.   class Inner extends java.awt.Color {
 6.      public void aaa() {
 7.         z = x + y + yMinus1();
 8.      }
 9.   }
10.
11.   private int yMinus1() { return y-1; }
12. }
```

Lines 1 and 5 show that the enclosing class and the inner class may extend any (non-final) superclasses. Line 7 shows code of the inner class accessing a private variable and a private method (z and yMinus1(), respectively) of the enclosing class.

The this pointer of an instance of an inner class provides access to the data and methods of the instance of the enclosing class that created the instance of the inner class. The following code provides an example:

```
 1. class Outer {
 2.    double dub;
 3.
 4.    void doSomething() {
 5.       dub = 1.234;
 6.       Inner inner = new Inner();
 7.       inner.resetDub();
 8.
 9.    class Inner {
10.       void resetDub() { dub = 0; }
11.    }
12. }
```

When an instance of class Outer executes its doSomething() method, the instance's dub is set to 1.234 (on line 5). Then an instance of Inner is created. This instance's this pointer can be used to reference the data of the creating instance of class Outer. Thus on line 10, the dub that gets reset to zero is the one owned by the current instance of Outer.

Inner Classes in Methods

An inner class may be defined within a method, known as the *enclosing method*. Such an inner class may only be used within the enclosing method.

An inner class within a method has access to all the data and methods of the enclosing class; additionally, it has access to all final arguments and data of the enclosing class. The following code shows an example of an inner class within a method:

```
1. class Outer {
2.    private int a;
3.
4.    void foo(double d, final float f) {
5.       String s;
6.       final boolean b;
7.
8.       class Inner {
9.          void methodInInner() { ... }
10.      }
11.   }
12. }
```

Class Inner is defined within method foo(). Code within the inner class (for example, in method methodInInner() on line 9) may access variables a, f, and b. a is accessible because it belongs to the enclosing class. f and b are accessible because they are final variables of the enclosing method. (f is a final argument; b is a final automatic variable.)

Anonymous Inner Classes

An anonymous inner class may only be defined within a method, so all of the restrictions reviewed in the previous section still apply. When you create an anonymous inner class, you do not give it a name, and you may only use it in one place in your code. The only way to construct an instance of an anonymous inner class is with the following syntax:

```
new Superclass_or_Interface(args_list) {class_
definition}
```

An anonymous inner class either extends a superclass or extends Object and implements a single interface (but not both). The name of the superclass or interface appears after the new keyword. Arguments to the constructor appear in the parenthetical argument list, which is followed by curly brackets that enclose the class definition.

The following code shows an example of an anonymous inner class that extends java.util.Vector:

```
1. import java.util.Vector;
2.
3. class Outer {
4.   void aaa() {
5.     Vector vec = new Vector() {
6.       public boolean add(Object ob) {
7.         System.out.println("ADDING " + ob);
8.         return super.add(ob);
9.       } // End of add() method
10.    };  // End of anonymous inner class def
11.    vec.add(this);
12.    vec.add(new Double(12.345));
13.    vec.add("Hello world.");
14.  }     // End of enclosing method
15. }      // End of class
```

The anonymous inner class is defined on lines 5–10. It overrides the add() method, making it verbose. The class is only used once, at construction time. (The value returned by the constructor is stored in vec, which is of type Vector. There is no way to have a reference variable whose type is an anonymous inner class.) The instance of the anonymous inner class is used three times, on lines 11–13.

The following code fragment illustrates an anonymous inner class that implements an interface (and thus, implicitly, extends Object). The interface is java.awt.event.ActionListener, which defines the single method public void actionPerformed(ActionEvent). This interface is a listener interface; listeners are reviewed in Chapter 8, "The java.awt Package."

```
1. import java.awt.*;
2. import java.awt.event.*;
3.
4. public class MyPanel extends Panel {
5.    public MyPanel() {
6.       Button btn = new Button("OK");
7.       btn.addActionListener(new ActionListener() {
8.        public void actionPerformed(ActionEvent e){
9.           System.out.println("OK");
10.       }  // End of method
11.     });  // End of anonymous inner class
12.   }       // End of constructor
13. }
```

The anonymous inner class is defined on lines 7–11.

Static Inner Classes

A static inner class, like a static method, has no this pointer and may not access the nonstatic data and methods of the enclosing class. The following example class contains a static inner class.

```
1. class Outer {
2.    int a, b;
3.    static int c, d;
4.
5.    void xxx()      { System.out.println("Hello")};
6.    static void yyy(){ System.out.println("Bye")};
7.
8.    static class StaticInner {
9.      void zzz() {
```

```
10.        c = d + 10;
11.          yyy();
12.      }
13.    }
14. }
```

The method zzz(), which is defined within the static inner class, may access variables c and d and call method yyy(), of the enclosing class. Variables a and b, and method xxx(), are not static, so they may not be accessed from the static inner class.

A static inner class may not be defined within a method.

Inner Classes from Static Code

When an instance of an inner class is constructed under ordinary circumstances, it receives a reference to the constructing instance of the enclosing class. However, when you want to construct an inner class from a static method, there is no instance of the enclosing class, and a different syntax must be used.

For example, consider an enclosing class named Outer that contains a nonstatic inner class named Inner. The only way a static method of Outer may construct and reference an instance of Inner is with the syntax shown on line 5.

```
1. class Outer {
2.    class Inner { }
3.
4.    static void staticMethod() {
5.      Outer.Inner oi = new Outer().new Inner();
6.    }
7. }
```

Exam Essentials

Know which data and methods of an enclosing class are available to an inner class. Understand that the inner class may access all data and methods of its enclosing class.

Be able to identify correctly constructed inner classes, including inner classes in methods, and anonymous inner classes. The syntax for each of these forms is explained in previous sections of this chapter.

Understand the restrictions on static inner classes. Understand that a static inner class may not access nonstatic features of its enclosing class.

Know how to use a nonstatic inner class from a static method of the enclosing class. Be able to recognize the new `Outer().new Inner()` format.

Key Terms and Concepts

Enclosing class   A class that contains an inner class.

Enclosing method   A method that contains an inner class.

Inner class   A class that is defined within another class.

Sample Questions

1. Which of the following kinds of inner classes are legal?

   A. An inner class that is defined in a method and reads a non-final variable of the enclosing class.

   B. An inner class that is defined in a method and reads a non-final variable of the enclosing method.

   C. A static inner class that calls a static method of the enclosing class.

D. A static inner class that calls a nonstatic method of the enclosing class.

Answer: A, C. A is legal because any inner class may read any variable of the enclosing class. B is illegal because an inner class in a method may only access the arguments and automatic variables of the method that are final. C is legal because the only methods of the enclosing class that may be called by a static inner class are the static methods. D is illegal for the same reason.

2. Which of the following kinds of inner classes are legal?

A. An anonymous inner class that extends the `java.util.Vector` class and implements the `java.awt.ActionListener` interface.

B. An anonymous inner class that implements the `java.awt.ActionListener` and `java.awt.KeyListener` interfaces.

C. An anonymous inner class that calls a private method of the enclosing class.

D. An anonymous inner class that reads a variable of the enclosing class that is defined as "`private static double d;`".

E. An anonymous inner class that reads a variable of the enclosing method that is defined as "`private static double d;`".

Answer: C, D. A and B are illegal because an anonymous inner class extends a single superclass or implements a single interface. C is legal because any inner class (including an anonymous one) may call any method of the enclosing class, regardless of the method's access mode. D is legal because any inner class may read any variable of the enclosing class, regardless of the variable's access mode. E is illegal because anonymous inner classes are always defined within methods, and inner classes in methods are restricted to accessing only the final arguments and variables of their enclosing methods. Moreover, methods may not contain static variables.

Chapter

7

Threads

SUN CERTIFIED PROGRAMMER FOR THE JAVA 2
PLATFORM EXAM OBJECTIVES COVERED IN
THIS CHAPTER:

- Write code to define, instantiate, and start new threads using both *java.lang.Thread* and *java .lang.Runnable.*

- Recognize conditions that might prevent a thread from executing.

- Write code using *synchronized, wait, notify,* and *notifyAll* to protect against concurrent access problems and to communicate between threads. Define the interaction between threads and between threads and object locks when executing *sychronized, wait, notify,* or *notifyAll.*

Java is a multithreaded programming language and a multithreaded execution environment. Because of this, competence with threads is even required from programmers who do not think the code they write will be threaded. Both the AWT and the Swing windowing toolkit execute in a multithreaded fashion because of the thread scheduling model. Therefore, even pure GUI programmers must be able to handle threads effectively.

Write code to define, instantiate, and start new threads using both *java.lang .Thread* and *java.lang.Runnable*.

This objective is intended to ensure that you have a clear grasp of the fundamentals of Java's threading capabilities. Using Thread or Runnable to create and launch threads is the basic mechanism by which all explicit threading in a Java program is started.

Critical Information

All threads start their execution in a run() method. The interface java.lang.Runnable declares this method. The run() method can be implemented either in a class written for the purpose or in a subclass of java.lang.Thread that overrides the implementation of the run() method provided in the Thread class.

The run() method's full signature is as follows:

```
public void run()
```

It cannot throw any checked exceptions because none are declared in the interface, and like all interface methods, it must be public.

New threads of execution are created when new Thread objects are created. If the code to be executed is provided by a separate class that implements Runnable, then an instance of the Runnable implementation should be passed into the Thread constructor. The new thread starts executing after the start() method of the Thread instance has been called. This is the case regardless of which class provided the run() method that the thread will execute.

The run() method is, first and foremost, just a method. It can be called directly, in which case it executes like any other method, in the calling thread. Every invocation of the run() method creates a unique set of local variables that have the lifetime of the method.

Exam Essentials

Know how to write and run code for a thread by implementing the interface java.lang.Runnable.   Create a class that implements the interface Runnable. The run() method of this class may be used as the start point for a new thread if a Thread object is constructed with the Runnable implementation as an argument to the constructor. To launch the new thread, the start() method of the Thread object should be called.

Know how to write and run code for a thread by extending the class java.lang.Thread.   Create a class that extends the Thread class. Create a run() method with the signature defined in the Runnable interface. Create an instance of the new Thread subclass and call the start() method to launch the new thread.

Know the significance and full prototype of the public void run() method declared in the interface java.lang.Runnable.   Learn the prototype "public void run()" by heart. Know that this is the only way to provide the body of a thread—even Thread does this. Recognize that run() is a method like any other and, if called directly, will execute like any other—without creating any new thread. Recognize that every invocation of run(), like any other method, has its own set of local variables.

Know the distinction between the **start()** method of the **Thread** class and the **run()** method of the **Runnable** interface. Recognize that run() is where the thread starts execution, and distinguish this from start(), which is the method that creates and launches the new thread.

Key Terms and Concepts

java.lang.Runnable The interface that defines the run() method.

java.lang.Thread The class that provides the new thread of execution. Thread implements Runnable.

public void run() The method declared by the Runnable interface. This method is the starting point for a new thread's execution.

public void start() The method in the Thread class that launches a new thread's execution.

Sample Questions

1. Which classes are suitable for creating a new thread of execution, so that the class shown provides the code the thread executes?

A.
```
public class X implements Runnable {
    public void run() {
      // code for the thread body goes here...
    }
}
```

B.
```
public class X implements Thread {
    public void run() {
      // code for the thread body goes here...
    }
}
```

C.
```
public class X extends Thread {
    public int run() {
      // code for the thread body goes here...
```

```
    }
  }

D. public class X implements Runnable {
     protected void run() {
       // code for the thread body goes here...
     }
  }

E. public class X extends Thread {
     public void run() {
       // code for the thread body goes here...
     }
  }

F. public class X {
     public void run() {
       // code for the thread body goes here...
     }
  }
```

Answer: A, E. A is a conventional Runnable declaration. B does not compile, since Thread is a class and should therefore be extended, not implemented. The code of C would compile, but since the public void run() method that implements the Runnable interface has not been overridden, the body of the public int run() method does not provide the code for the thread. D is illegal, since all interface methods, including the run() method of Runnable, must be public. E is a conventional extension of Thread. F does not implement the Runnable interface, although it provides the method that is declared by Runnable. The implementation must be explicit.

2. Consider this code:

```
1. public class X extends Thread
      implements Runnable {
2.   public void run() {
3.     System.out.println("In run()");
4.   }
```

```
5.    public static void main(String [] args) {
6.      Thread t = new Thread(new X());
7.      t.start();
8.    }
9.  }
```

Which is/are true?

A. Line 1 causes a compilation error.

B. Line 6 causes a compilation error.

C. Line 6 causes a runtime error.

D. The program runs and starts two new threads.

E. The program runs and starts one new thread.

Answer: E. `Thread` implements `Runnable`, and although the `implements` clause on line 1 is redundant, it is not wrong. When the program runs, the "`new X()`" that forms the argument to the `Thread` constructor on line 6 is taken as a `Runnable`. Consequently, the `run()` method defined at lines 2 through 4 forms the body of the new thread of execution, which results from the `Thread` object that variable t refers to.

Recognize conditions that might prevent a thread from executing.

This objective is intended to ensure that you are aware of the issues that control the execution of a thread. In particular, an appreciation of the reasons for which a thread's execution can be suspended will allow you to recognize the lack of control that the programmer has over thread execution in many cases.

Critical Information

Threads can become non-runnable for a variety of reasons, and they can be paused even when still runnable for other reasons. In a JVM that is running more threads than the number of physical CPUs, some threads that are runnable must in fact be waiting a turn on a CPU. In addition, some threads will be unable to run for some reason.

Several methods might overtly pause the execution of a thread. These are wait(), sleep(), and yield(). Also, entering a synchronized region might force the thread to pause until it can obtain an object lock.

The methods suspend() and stop() are deprecated, and although they cause a thread to pause, or stop altogether, you should not use them, and they do not arise in the Certification Exam.

Threads can be paused for less explicit reasons than just the code they execute. At any time, thread scheduling can cause a thread to be taken off the CPU and paused, even if the thread is still in the runnable state. This can occur in both time-sliced and preemptive scheduling environments. In a time-sliced environment, from time to time the scheduler will stop execution of a runnable thread in favor of some other thread that has not run for a while. With a preemptive environment, if a thread becomes runnable and that thread is of higher priority than the currently running thread, then the scheduler will run the higher priority thread instead.

Many library methods can cause a thread to be paused. Typically, any thread that performs I/O (such as reading from a file or URL) or any method that has a word like "wait" in its name is a contender for pausing the calling thread.

Deadlock is a particularly effective, if undesirable, way that threads can be prevented from executing. The classic example of deadlock is *deadly embrace*. This occurs when two threads both block waiting for something that the other holds (in Java, these somethings might be object locks). In this situation, ordering can make all the difference. Consider two threads, A and B, both trying to synchronize on two objects, x and y. If they both try to obtain locks in the same order, then no problem can arise. By contrast, if thread A has a lock on x and then tries to lock y, while thread B has already gotten a lock on y and tries to get a lock on x, then deadly embrace results.

Exam Essentials

Know the mechanisms that explicitly suspend a thread's execution.
These mechanisms are entering any `synchronized` region, or calling `wait()`, `sleep()`, or `yield()`. You can ignore the deprecated methods for the exam.

Recognize indirect mechanisms that might suspend a thread's execution. Several indirect mechanisms might cause a thread to suspend execution. The scheduler might select another thread to run, because of either time-slicing or preemption. Calling any method that might need to use synchronization or interthread communication, or perform any kind of I/O operation, might result in a thread suspending. Also, any method with the word "`wait`" in its name might reasonably cause suspension.

Recognize code that might cause deadly embrace. Deadlock conditions cause permanent suspension of threads, and deadly embrace is the classic example of this.

Key Terms and Concepts

Deadlock A state where thread(s) are in a non-runnable state, waiting for a situation that is guaranteed not to occur because the thread is not running.

Deadly embrace The classic example of deadlock, in which two threads are waiting for resources, but each thread already holds the resource required by the other.

Non-runnable The state of a thread that cannot make use of a CPU even if one is available to it. An example is a thread that is waiting for data from an I/O device.

Preemption   A thread-scheduling approach that depends mainly upon interactions between related threads to make the most efficient use of available CPU time.

Runnable   The state of a thread that can use a CPU if one is available. Nothing within the thread's state prevents it from making useful computational progress.

sleep()   A static method in the Thread class that makes the calling thread non-runnable for a specified period of time.

Thread scheduling   The way decisions are made about which thread will execute on a CPU at any given instant.

Time-slicing   A thread-scheduling approach that shares CPU time more or less evenly between multiple threads.

wait()   A method in the Object class that makes a thread non-runnable until explicit intervention (the notify() method) from another thread.

yield()   A static method in the Thread class that makes the calling thread non-runnable for an instant if other threads are runnable.

Sample Questions

1. Which of the following can be the direct cause of a thisThread becoming blocked? Assume the variable thisThread refers to the thread that might block and thatThread refers to another thread.

   A. thatThread executes thisThread.sleep(1000);.

   B. thisThread executes thatThread.sleep(1000);.

   C. thisThread attempts to read from a file.

   D. thisThread executes new Thread(someRunnable);.

   E. thisThread raises its own priority.

Answer: B, C. The sleep() method is static and always acts on the currently executing thread. So, even though A looks like it should affect thisThread, and B looks like it should affect thatThread, the calling thread always blocks, so B is a correct answer. C is also correct because reading from a file is I/O and is likely to block at least for a short while, until the data are available from the disk. Creating a new thread doesn't block the current one; even starting it doesn't really block it directly. It's fair to say, however, that either creating or starting might nudge the scheduling enough to indirectly block the current thread. Raising the priority of a thread will not directly cause it to block, although lowering the priority might, depending upon the scheduling algorithm.

2. Consider the following method:

```
public void twoLocks(Object a, Object b) {
  synchronized(a) {
    synchronized(b) {
      // do something with a and b
    }
  }
}
```

and the following instantiations:

```
Object p = new Object();
Object q = new Object();
```

Both are in scope for two different threads that are about to call the twoLocks() method. Assume the first thread calls twoLocks(p, q). Which is true?

A. The second thread should call twoLocks(p, q).

B. The second thread should call twoLocks(q, p).

C. The second thread should not call the twoLocks() method until it is certain the first thread has completed the method.

D. The second thread can call the twoLocks() method at any time with the arguments in any order.

Answer: A. Calling the method with the arguments in reversed order is susceptible to deadly embrace. Calling the method after the first thread has completed the method is safe but unnecessarily cautious. Since B is subject to deadly embrace, D is also untrue.

Write code using *synchronized, wait, notify,* and *notifyAll* to protect against concurrent access problems and to communicate between threads. Define the interaction between threads and between threads and object locks when executing *sychronized, wait, notify,* or *notifyAll.*

This objective is intended to ensure you have a clear grasp of thread interactions. Generally, as soon as multiple threads are started—if those threads have any interaction at all—you will find that you need to understand these issues. Failure to do so will cause some very strange, often inconsistent or unrepeatable, problems.

Critical Information

Java provides a mechanism for interthread communication and control, including protection of critical sections of code to ensure data integrity in concurrent access situations. The methods wait(), notify(), and notifyAll(), along with the synchronized keyword, are the elements of this mechanism.

wait() and *notify()* Methods and Interthread Communication

The methods wait() and notify() form the core of the interthread communication mechanism. Viewed simplistically, one thread uses the wait() method to block until another thread issues a notify() call that causes the first thread to proceed. There is a little more detail, however, which will be discussed in the following paragraphs.

A thread must hold an object's lock prior to attempting to execute any of the methods wait(), notify(), and notifyAll() on that object. If this is not the case, an exception is thrown.

To obtain the lock, the thread must enter a synchronized block. Only one thread can be actively executing in a synchronized block in the context of a single object at one time. This exclusion is managed using a concept of locks. The effect (but possibly not the implementation) is that each object has a "lock" associated with it. To execute the synchronized keyword, a thread must obtain the lock. If the lock is already held by another thread, then the thread attempting to execute the synchronized keyword must block until the lock is available.

A synchronized block can occur in one of two forms. It can either be a synchronized method, or a block that starts as follows:

```
synchronized(target) {
```

where target is a reference to the object in question. Commonly, target would actually be this.

When a thread executes the wait() method on an object, it must initially hold the lock. This usually means the wait() method call occurs inside a synchronized block, but it is possible, albeit error-prone and inelegant, to depend on the lock already being held as a result of a synchronized block in the calling method, or some other method further up the caller hierarchy.

When a thread executes the wait() method, it gives up the lock and becomes non-runnable and blocked, waiting for a notification. When the notification comes, the thread does not become runnable; rather, it moves to another blocked state waiting to regain the object lock. Because the thread must regain the lock before it continues executing, the rule stating that only one thread can be "actively executing in a synchronized block in the context of a single object at one time" is upheld.

Notification is issued by another thread executing either the notify() or notifyAll() method. To do this, the notifying thread must hold the object lock (this is one compelling reason for the thread that executes wait() to release the lock). This is why it is certain that the lock is not available to any waiting threads at the instant the notify() method call occurs.

If multiple threads are waiting on the same object, there is no guarantee as to which will be moved from the waiting state into the waiting-for-lock state. In many implementations, the ordering is FIFO (first to wait is first to wake up), but this is *not* a specification requirement, and it is important to avoid writing code that depends upon this behavior.

The notifyAll() method causes all threads that are waiting on an object to move from the waiting state to the waiting-for-lock state. Of course, only one at a time can obtain the lock and continue execution.

Interthread communication can be implemented very simply using wait() and notify() to enable one thread to set up some data and then pass that data to another thread by calling notify() while the receiver thread is in the wait() method. In simple cases of this communication style, critical sections will often be protected by the need to make the calls to wait() and notify() inside synchronized blocks.

Static methods can be marked synchronized, as can ordinary methods. In this case, the lock is taken from the class object, rather than the object instance. This means that static synchronized methods cannot be concurrently actively executing in the context of the same class, but a static synchronized method and a synchronized instance method of the same class can be concurrently executing. This is comparable to concurrently executing the same synchronized block in the context of two different instances. In both cases, two different locks are involved, and both threads proceed unimpeded.

Protection of Critical Sections

You must use synchronized blocks to protect critical sections of code. In general, any piece of code that puts data through invalid states during a multistep update forms a critical section. Consider this simple example that represents a rectangle:

```
1. public class Rectangle {
2.    private int x, y;
3.    private int w, h;
4.
5.    public void setSize(int w, int h) {
6.       this.w = w;
7.       this.h = h;
8.    }
9. }
```

This class is actually not threadsafe. Consider what happens if two threads execute the setSize() method concurrently. Acceptable results would be for the values set by one or the other thread to be adopted. This might not be the case, however.

Imagine that thread A is trying to set a width of 2 and a height of 2, while thread B is trying to set both dimensions to 4. Thread A has executed line 6 but not yet line 7, when the vagaries of thread scheduling cause thread B to take over the CPU, putting thread A on hold (common in a time-sliced environment). Now thread B executes the whole of the setSize() method. At this point, both the width and height of the rectangle are set at 4. Finally, however, thread A is rescheduled, carries on where it left off, executes line 7, and sets the height of the rectangle to 2. Now we have data that are not valid from either thread, and it is generally accepted that the rectangle has been corrupted.

To protect against this kind of corruption in situations where threading is possible, it is normal to make any multistep updates to data part of a synchronized block. So, the example would be modified as one of the two following examples:

```
5.    public synchronized void setSize(int w, int h) {
6.        this.w = w;
7.        this.h = h;
8.    }
```
or
```
5.    public void setSize(int w, int h) {
6.        synchronized(this) {
7.          this.w = w;
8.          this.h = h;
9.        }
10.   }
```

An important consideration is that this type of protection only works if all write access to the sensitive variables (w and h, in this case) is protected. Further, to be sure the protection is enforced, the variables that are protected must be private, otherwise they can be updated improperly from outside the class.

The method run() is a method just like any other, and it has its own local variables that are distinct for every invocation. This is an important point because member variables are not subject to corruption by concurrent thread access; every time a method is invoked, whether by one thread or by several, a new set of local variables is created. This means that member variables, not method locals, give rise to critical sections.

Exam Essentials

Know that a thread must hold an object's lock before it calls notify(), notifyAll(), or wait() on that object. Attempting to call any of these methods without holding the lock causes an exception.

Know that calling **wait()** releases the object lock and makes the thread non-runnable. Otherwise no other thread could obtain that lock, which is needed to execute notify().

Know and recognize the significance of the fact that a newly notified thread (one that was previously waiting) must regain the object's lock before it becomes runnable. Any thread that receives a notify while in a wait pool definitely does not become runnable immediately.

Know that the resumption order of threads that execute **wait()** on an object is not specified. Despite the fact that many implementations give FIFO behavior to threads waiting on an object, the specification states that the resumption order is unspecified.

Recognize critical sections of code in a method. Know that multistep data updates have critical sections. Any divisible data modification has potential for a critical section. Unexpected thread behavior (due to time-slicing, for example) can cause context switches between threads at any time.

Know how to use private access and the **synchronized** keywords to protect critical sections. The synchronized keyword does not prevent threads from context switching; instead, it prevents other threads from accessing the same object lock concurrently. Variables that are not private are accessible from some other classes; those classes might not implement proper protection of critical sections.

Key Terms and Concepts

Critical section A piece of code that could cause data corruption if another thread executes concurrently in the same context.

notify() The method in the Object class that causes a (randomly chosen) thread that is waiting on this object to be moved from the waiting state into the waiting-for-lock state.

notifyAll() The method in the Object class that causes all threads that are waiting on this object to be moved from the waiting state into the waiting-for-lock state.

Object lock   The flag that is used to implement exclusivity between threads. One object lock exists for every object instance in a JVM, and each lock can be associated with either its owning object or a single thread. Note that the flag might not be "real," but it accurately describes the behavior that the JVM provides.

synchronized   The keyword that indicates that prior to entering the next block, the executing thread must hold the lock on the relevant object. In the case of a synchronized instance method, the relevant object is this. In the case of a static synchronized method, the relevant object is the java.lang.Class object of the class that defines the method. In the case of a synchronized block, the relevant object is explicitly named in the argument part of the synchronized call.

Threadsafe   A class that has been written in such a way that no matter how many threads execute concurrently, and how they are scheduled by the system, the data of the instances will definitely remain valid.

wait()   The method in the Object class that causes a thread to suspend execution and give up the object lock, pending notification from another thread on the same object. Often used to implement a listener behavior in a communication mechanism.

Waiting-for-lock   The state of a thread that needs to obtain the object lock to become runnable.

Sample Questions

1. Which methods may be called by any thread at any time?

   A. notify()

   B. wait()

   C. notifyAll()

   D. sleep()

   E. yield()

   F. synchronized(this)

Answer: D, E, F. wait(), notify(), and notifyAll() may only be called by a thread that holds the lock of the object on which the method is invoked.

2. Which is true of a thread that is blocked inside a wait() method call?

   A. The thread holds an object lock.

   B. The thread does not hold an object lock.

   C. The thread might hold an object lock.

   Answer: B. Although the thread must hold the lock before it executes the wait() method, it releases it before it blocks. After notification, the thread waits to regain the lock. As it regains the lock, it becomes runnable.

3. Three threads execute wait() on the same object. Which approach can be used to ensure that when notify() calls are made to the object, the waiting threads resume activity in the same order as they executed the wait() method?

   A. The threads are guaranteed to resume in this order naturally; nothing needs to be done.

   B. Nothing can be done to cause this ordering.

   C. The situation is moot; only one thread can wait on a single object.

   D. The situation is moot because all three threads will resume at once.

   E. Send a notifyAll() instead of a notify().

Answer: B. In many JVMs, this happens to be the natural order of resumption, but it is also a platform-dependent behavior that cannot be safely relied upon. Multiple threads can wait on the same object; if not, the notifyAll() method would have no value. D describes an approximation to the effect of notifyAll(). However, even notifyAll() does not cause all the threads to resume at once, because upon receiving a notification, a thread moves from blocked waiting to blocked waiting for the object lock. This means that only one can possibly become runnable, and it can only do so when it gets the lock.

4. Assume you are writing a piece of code in which two variables, x and y, should maintain a particular relationship. You want to protect the relationship against damage due to concurrent access by multiple threads. Which statements are correct?

   A. The variables should be marked protected.

   B. The variables should be marked private.

   C. The variables can have any accessibility.

   D. All methods of the class must be synchronized.

   E. All methods that have access to the variables must be synchronized.

   Answer: B. If the variables are accessible by code outside of the class, then no guarantee can be made that only the correct algorithms coded in this class will be able to modify the variables. The critical sections of all methods that manipulate the variables should be contained in synchronized blocks. However, these synchronized blocks do not necessarily have to extend over the entire method, so D and E are not true because they might be excessive. Although B alone will not guarantee the safety of the variables, it is the only choice that is actually correct, which is what the question asks for. The question does not ask what must be done to protect the relationship.

Chapter

8

The *java.awt* Package

SUN CERTIFIED PROGRAMMER FOR JAVA 2
PLATFORM EXAM OBJECTIVES COVERED IN
THIS CHAPTER:

▶ Write code using *Component, Container,* and *LayoutManager* classes of the *java.awt* package to present a GUI with the specified appearance and resize behavior, and distinguish the responsibilities of layout managers from those of containers.

▶ Write code to implement listener classes and methods, and in listener methods, extract information from the event to determine the affected component, mouse position, nature, and time of the event. State the event classname for any specified event listener in the *java.awt.event* package.

You should be conversant with the basic operation of the Abstract Window Toolkit (AWT) because, even if you use another window library to create GUIs, the basic principles of AWT are common to other libraries. In addition, even if you generally do not write UI code, you should have a basic knowledge of how to do this; otherwise your horizons will be severely limited.

Write code using *Component, Container,* and *Layout Manager* classes of the *java.awt* package to present a GUI with the specified appearance and resize behavior, and distinguish the responsibilities of layout managers from those of containers.

This objective is intended to ensure you have a clear grasp of the basics of building and laying out a GUI. Java uses layout managers to control the size and position of components in a layout, so these are an essential part of any layout.

Critical Information

You should understand two essential topics relating to this objective: adding components to containers, and laying out components with layout managers. The most important information about layout managers is the behavior, or policy, that each implements. Before delving into this topic, however, we will address the issues of containers and components.

Containers and Components

Containers provide screen area for components; all components except top-level containers (`Frame`, `Dialog`, `Window`) must be placed in a container if they are to be visible. This applies to non-top-level containers, too.

The constructors for `Frame` take either zero arguments or a title string. A `Window` requires a parent, which may be either another `Window` or a `Frame`. For `Dialog`, several permutations exist. Each takes a reference to either a frame or dialog that is the "owner" of the dialog (and determines its position). A title string is also optional, as is a flag indicating if the dialog is modal. Modal dialogs grab all input from the application, but not from other applications, until closed.

Containers (`Container`, `Panel`, and `Applet` classes) are components, so containers can contain containers. This allows the building of arbitrarily deep containment hierarchies. The containment hierarchy is a runtime structure that is distinguished from the class hierarchy of the component classes themselves. The constructors for `Container` and `Applet` take no arguments; for `Panel`, a layout manager may be specified.

To add a component to a container, several `add()` methods are provided in the `Container` class. You should know two methods well for the certification exam, `add(Component)` and `add(Component, Object)`. The first method is used to put components into a layout where only the order of adding is significant—this includes the flow and grid layouts. The second method is used when it is necessary to pass additional information that the layout manager may use to assist in positioning the component. This includes the border, card, and grid bag layouts. The second argument is called the constraints object.

Containers delegate the work of component layout to `LayoutManager` objects. Layout managers avoid the need for you to work with pixel positioning, which would be platform dependent. Instead, they perform layout according to a policy. A layout manager's policy defines a general set of layout capabilities, and within those, the programmer is afforded some level of control over the way the components are laid out. The available control varies from minimal to extensive.

Every container has a default layout manager; top-level containers (Frame, Dialog, and Window) use a BorderLayout by default, while other containers (Panel, Applet) use a FlowLayout by default. If the default layout manager is not suitable, another may be used by calling the container's setLayout(LayoutManager) method.

FlowLayout Policy

FlowLayout lays out components in a manner similar to the layout of English words on a page. Each component has its preferred, or natural, size, and the separate components run from left to right in a horizontal row as wide as the container allows. When the row is full, components are positioned on a new line below the previous one.

The rows of components may be flushed left or right, or may be centered, based on a constructor argument. The default is to center the components.

Components are generally added to a container that uses flow layout with the container's add(Component) method, since the constraints object does not affect the component's size or position.

BorderLayout Policy

BorderLayout divides the container it operates with into five regions. These regions are generally referred to using constants that are defined in the BorderLayout class. The main constant names are NORTH, SOUTH, EAST, WEST, and CENTER. Each region, if used, contains only one component, although that component may be a container.

The north and south regions each force their component to the full width of the container and the component's own preferred height. The east and west regions give their components their preferred width but force their height to fill the vertical gap between north and south. The center region makes its component take up the remaining space.

Components are generally added to a container that uses a border layout with the add(Component, Object) method of the container. The object argument is the constant that defines the region to which the component is to be added.

GridLayout Policy

GridLayout divides its region into the number of rows and columns specified by the constructor arguments. All components are forced to the same dimensions, regardless of their preferred size. The dimensions are determined by dividing the available space into a grid of equally sized rectangles, based on the number of rows and columns specified when the grid layout was constructed. The first argument to a GridLayout constructor is the number of rows, and the second is the number of columns.

Components are generally added to a container that is using a grid layout with the add(Component) method, since the component's position in the grid is determined by the sequence of adding, rather than by the constraints object. Components are added to the layout from left to right to fill a row, and the rows are filled from top to bottom.

CardLayout Policy

The CardLayout policy lays components out in time rather than in space. One component may be selected at a time. Methods are provided to allow selection of components on a next/previous basis or by name. Each component is sized to entirely fill the space available in the container.

Components are commonly added to a container that is using a card layout using the add(Component, Object) method of the container, so the constraint object (typically a String) may be used to select a particular component for display. If it is only necessary to cycle through components in order, then the add(Component) method may be used instead.

GridBagLayout Policy

The GridBagLayout policy allows complex layouts and can imitate both border and grid layouts, and a single line of flow layout. It uses rows and columns of potentially unequal sizes as the basis of the layout.

Components are assigned to regions; each region is a rectangle composed of one or more contiguous cells in the grid structure. Components can take their natural size or be constrained to the full width, height, or both, of their allotted region. If a component does not fill its region, it can be positioned in the center of the region, in the center of any edge, or in any corner.

When the container is resized, the excess space is allocated to rows and columns in proportions governed by the weight assigned to the rows and columns. Rows or columns with a zero width remain unchanged, while the available change is divided between the other rows or columns according to the ratio of applicable weight to the total weight in that dimension. For example, if 200 pixels of horizontal stretch are being shared, and four columns have weights of 1, 2, 3, and 4, then the first column would get 20 pixels, the second 40, the third 60, and the final column, with a weight of 4, would get 80 pixels.

Where a container is using a grid bag layout, an instance of the class `GridBagConstraints` is provided as the constraints object when the component is added to the container. Therefore, components are added to a container that is using a grid bag layout using the `add(Component, Object)` method of the container class. The grid bag constraints object conveys information about how the component should be treated. The fields are public, and the most important ones are as follows:

int anchor Indicates the position in the available region if the component does not fill the region.

int fill Indicates whether the component should fill the region horizontally, vertically, both, or neither.

int gridheight Indicates how many rows are part of a component's region.

int gridwidth Indicates how many columns are part of a component's region.

int gridx Indicates the leftmost column that is part of a component's region.

int gridy Indicates the top row that is part of a component's region.

double weightx   Indicates the proportion of size change that should be applied to this column when the container is resized.

double weighty   Indicates the proportion of size change that should be applied to this row when the container is resized.

An often misunderstood point is that, although a weightx and weighty field exists in every GridBagConstraints object and is therefore associated with every component added to a container with a grid bag layout, the weight values actually apply to the rows and columns as a whole and not to the components. Public arrays in the GridBagLayout object allow these values to be set explicitly, rather than passing them in "piggy-backed" on a component.

Exam Essentials

Know how to create a top-level container and add components and containers to it.   The basic construction of a Frame or Dialog, followed by construction of other components and containers, is essential to understand. Add components using the appropriate add() method.

Know how to enforce a particular layout manager upon a container.   Use the setLayout(LayoutManager) method of the Container class.

Know the default layout managers associated with containers. Top-level containers (Frame, Dialog, and Window) have a border layout by default. Other containers get a flow layout by default.

Know the policy of each layout manager and recognize the effect of each on the sizes of components.   Does a layout manager govern the size of a component or take some account of the preferred size? Where are components placed and how are they resized if the container size changes? What constraints can or should be applied when a component is added, and what effect do those constraints have?

Key Terms and Concepts

BorderLayout   The default layout manager for top-level containers (frame and dialog). The policy of this layout manager uses five regions and puts one component into each region.

CardLayout   This layout manager displays one component at a time in the full space of the container. Components can be selected for display one at a time from the full set of added components.

Component   A parent class of all elements of a Java GUI.

Container   A subclass of component that is able to provide screen space to other components, including other containers.

Constraints object   An object that describes how a component should be laid out. The object is passed with the component in the add(Component, Object) method of the Container class.

FlowLayout   The default layout manager for panels and applets. This layout manager has a policy that positions components on lines in a fashion similar to the words of English text on a page.

GridBagConstraints   The class that carries configuration information with a component to control how the component is sized and positioned by a grid bag layout.

GridBagLayout   The most complex layout manager. Components are laid out in regions composed of one or more cells in an irregular grid. The width of individual columns and the height of individual rows can change when the container is resized. The changes are governed by the relative weight of each.

GridLayout   This layout manager divides the container into equally sized rows and equally sized columns. Each contained component is forced to the full size of a resulting grid section.

LayoutManager   The interface that provides for the ability to control size and position of components in a container.

Layout policy   The rules by which a layout manager sets the size and position of components. Each layout manager has its own policy. The use of policy-based layout avoids the need for platform-dependent pixel-by-pixel specifications.

Top-level container   A frame, dialog, or window object. These containers can be made visible without being added to any other container.

Weight   The element that controls how a row's height or a column's width change as the container's size changes.

Sample Questions

1. Which components border the left edge of this layout?

```
public class MyLayout extends Frame {
  public MyLayout() {
    add(new Label("One"), BorderLayout.WEST);
    add(new Label("Two"), BorderLayout.SOUTH);
    add(new Label("Three"), BorderLayout.CENTER);
    add(new Label("Four"), BorderLayout.EAST);
  }
}
```

A. Label "One"

B. Label "Two"

C. Label "Three"

D. Label "Four"

Answer: A, B. Label "Three" is kept away from the left edge by label "One". Label "Four" is entirely at the right of the layout. The layout manager is border by default for a Frame.

2. Which components in this layout resize horizontally when the container is resized?

```java
public class MyLayout extends Frame {
  public MyLayout() {
    add(new Label("One"), BorderLayout.WEST);
    add(new Label("Two"), BorderLayout.SOUTH);
    add(new Label("Three"), BorderLayout.CENTER);
    add(new Label("Four"), BorderLayout.EAST);
  }
}
```

A. Label "One"

B. Label "Two"

C. Label "Three"

D. Label "Four"

Answer: B, C. The layout manager is border by default for a Frame; components in the north, center, and south regions are affected horizontally. Components in the east, center, and west are affected vertically.

3. Which layout managers are able to alter a component's horizontal size without affecting the vertical size, given that the container has been resized in both directions?

A. Flow

B. Border

C. Grid

D. Card

E. GridBag

Answer: B, E. Flow does not resize its components. Grid and card resize all components equally in both dimensions when the container changes in both. Components in the north and south of a border layout are affected horizontally but never vertically. Each component, and each dimension of each component, may be controlled individually in grid bag.

4. Which layout managers are able to allow a component to have its preferred size?

   A. Flow

   B. Border

   C. Grid

   D. Card

   E. GridBag

   Answer: A, E. Border constrains at least one dimension of all components it contains. Grid and card constrain both. Flow never constrains either dimension, while GridBag gives you full control of this on a component-by-component basis.

5. Which fields of `GridBagLayout` can affect the width of a component?

   A. anchor

   B. fill

   C. gridwidth

   D. gridx

   E. weightx

   Answer: B, C, E. The `fill` field can cause a component to adopt the width, height, or both of the cell it is assigned to, or allow it to adopt a preferred dimension. The `gridwidth` field affects the size of the cell in which the component is positioned; if `fill` is not NONE, this can affect the width. The `weightx` field affects the distribution of space when a container is not at the preferred size of the whole layout; again, if `fill` is not NONE, this can affect the size of the component.

6. Which classes contain code that determines the appropriate size or position of components?

A. FlowLayout

B. Panel

C. Button

D. CheckboxGroup

E. GridBagLayout

Answer: A, E. The size and position of components is the responsibility of layout managers, not containers or components. (The Component class contains methods that set the size and/or position, but only in response to externally supplied parameters. The component does not make any decisions about what the size or position should be.) CheckboxGroup is a logical grouping that enforces radio button–style behavior among checkboxes; it has no influence over the UI presentation.

Write code to implement listener classes and methods, and in listener methods, extract information from the event to determine the affected component, mouse position, nature, and time of the event. State the event classname for any specified event listener in the *java.awt.event* package.

This objective is intended to ensure you understand the fundamentals of event handling. The event mechanism provides the tools with which a program's behavior is attached to user inputs.

Critical Information

In the AWT since JDK 1.1, events are delivered to explicitly registered listeners. There are four key parts to the system: the event source, the listener, the interface the listener must implement, and the event object that is delivered.

When the appropriate stimulus occurs, the event source creates objects of the appropriate event class and then delivers that event to each registered listener by calling the appropriate handler method of the listener.

Listener Interfaces, Adapter Classes, and Event Class Names

Events are grouped into categories, and for each category, a listener interface is provided that must be implemented by any object that needs to receive events of that category. Some of the listener interfaces declare only a single handler method, but others declare two or more. For all interfaces that have more than a single method, an adapter is also provided. The *adapter* classes all implement the related listener interface using handler methods with empty bodies. Therefore, to use an adapter, at least one method must be overridden. By contrast, to use a listener interface, all the declared methods must be implemented.

In any interface, all methods are public. All event handler methods return void. In each individual listener interface, all the event handler methods take a single argument of the same event type. The event type name is usually derived directly from the listener interface name. For example, the handler methods of the `MouseListener` interface all take a `MouseEvent`. This general mapping holds true for all listeners except `MouseMotionListener`. In this case, the event type is actually `MouseEvent`, rather than mouse motion event.

Obtaining Information about the Event

Each event class carries information that might be useful in the handler method. This information describes aspects of the original occurrence that caused the event to be sent. One of the most important things that an event handler must know is why the event was issued. Generally, since JDK 1.1, this has been implicit in the handler method that is called. Additionally, a method, getID(), is defined in the AWTEvent class and might occasionally be useful for determining the reason for this event.

NOTE   The primary function of the getID() method is to simplify dispatching of events inside the source object itself. This is done by the processEvent() method but is beyond what is required for the exam.

Other information about the event varies with the actual event, but the getX(), getY(), and getPoint() methods of the MouseEvent class indicate where a mouse press, release, or click event occurred.

The time at which an event occurred is available for instances of InputEvent. InputEvent is a common parent class of both the KeyEvent and MouseEvent classes. The method that accesses this information is getWhen().

Exam Essentials

Know how to implement a specified interface, either by subclassing the adapter or by implementing the interface directly. Know how to implement either of these approaches with an anonymous inner class.   All listener methods in an interface take the same event type, which is derived from the listener interface name. All listener methods are public and return void. For all AWT listener interfaces that have more than one handler method, there is an adapter class.

Know the accessor methods of the events that identify the affected component, mouse position, nature, and time of the event.   The getSource(), getX(), getY(), getID(), and getWhen() methods provide this information. Generally, the reason for an event is implicit in the handler method that has been invoked.

Know or derive the event name used in every listener.   Most events are directly derived from the listener name, the exception being `MouseMotionListener`, which reuses the `MouseEvent`.

Key Terms and Concepts

Adapter   In the AWT, the adapter classes are no-behavior implementations of some listener interfaces.

Event   An object that carries information describing what happened when an event source calls a handler method in a listener.

Event source   An object that can call handler methods in a listener to indicate that something of interest has occurred.

Handler method   One of the methods declared by a listener interface.

Listener   An object that wishes to receive events of a particular category. A listener must implement the appropriate listener interface to be added to the event source.

`Listener` **interface**   In the AWT, an interface that declares the handler methods for a particular category of events.

Sample Questions

1. Which class is used for the argument of the handler method in an `ActionListener`?

   A. `Action`

   B. `ActionListener`

   C. `ActionHandler`

   D. `ActionEvent`

   E. `ActionPerformed`

Answer: D. Event names, with one exception, may be determined by dropping the "Listener" part of the interface name and replacing it with "Event". The exception is for the Mouse-MotionListener, which simply uses the MouseEvent.

2. In a MouseListener handler, how would you determine the position at which a mouse click occurs?

   A. Call the method getPosition() on the MouseEvent.

   B. Call the getX() method on the MouseEvent.

   C. Call the getY() method on the MouseEvent.

   D. Call the getSource() method in the event, then call the getX() and getY() methods in that object.

   E. This is not possible; position is tracked using the MouseMotionListener interface.

   Answer: B and C. There is no method called getPosition(), although there is a method called getPoint() in the MouseEvent class. The methods getX() and getY() are also defined in that class. This makes B and C correct. The methods are not defined in the source object, which would be a Component of some sort. E is untrue; MouseMotionListener is used to track position during movement, not when a click occurs.

3. Which may be used to determine information about the reason an event was issued from inside a handler method?

   A. Call the method getID() on the event object.

   B. Use a switch statement on the event object class.

   C. This information is implicit in the handler method that is being run.

   D. Consult the event registrations list in the event source.

   E. Use the instanceof operator on the event source.

Answer: A and C. A switch statement cannot be applied to any value that is not assignment-compatible with int. This rules out class comparisons. The registrations in an event source are not generally visible outside the class and would not identify the reason anyway. Using instanceof on the event source might give some assistance but would be indirect and probably inconclusive, since one object can often source multiple event classes. Generally, in the 1.1 event model you know the reason for the event by the handler you are in. However, the getID() method does carry information and might be useful in some situations.

4. Which class is used for the argument of the handler method in a MouseMotionListener?

   A. Mouse

   B. MouseMotionListener

   C. MouseMotionHandler

   D. MouseMotionEvent

   E. MouseEvent

   Answer: E. MouseMotionListener is the exception to the general rule that describes event names in handler methods.

Chapter

9

The *java.lang* Package

**SUN CERTIFIED PROGRAMMER FOR JAVA 2
PLATFORM EXAM OBJECTIVES COVERED IN
THIS CHAPTER:**

▶ Write code using the following methods of the
java.lang.Math class: *abs(), ceil(), floor(), max(),
min(), random(), round(), sin(), cos(), tan(), sqrt().*

▶ Describe the significance of the immutability of
String objects.

The java.lang package is fundamental and essential. This doesn't mean it's easy (although, compared to the other material in this book, it is relatively easy). It means there is no escaping java.lang. These objectives make sure you are up to speed on the functions of some of the package's major classes.

Write code using the following methods of the *java.lang.Math* class: *abs(), ceil(), floor(), max(), min(), random(), round(), sin(), cos(), tan(), sqrt()*.

The java.lang.Math class is a final class. Its constructor is private (thus you can never construct an instance), and all its methods are static. This is as close as you ever get in Java to a traditional library of functions. Since the Math class resides in the java.lang package, it is always imported automatically. You will be expected to be familiar with all the methods listed in this objective.

Critical Information

In the following sections we will review each of the methods mentioned in the objective. There are many other methods in java.lang .Math, but these are the ones you are most likely to encounter.

The *abs()* Method

The abs() method returns the absolute value of its single argument. If the argument is positive or zero, the return value is the same as the argument. If the argument is negative, the return value is the negative of the argument (hence a positive number). Thus an absolute value is always zero or positive. Table 9.1 shows some examples of absolute values.

TABLE 9.1:   Absolute Values

x	Absolute Value of x
–5	5
0	0
5	5

The abs() method is overloaded. There are four versions, as follows:

- `public static int abs(int x)`
- `public static long abs(long x)`
- `public static float abs(float x)`
- `public static double abs(double x)`

In each case, the return type matches the argument type.

The *ceil()* and *floor()* Methods

The ceil() and floor() methods both take double arguments and have double return types. The return value is always an integer expressed as a double. In both cases, if the argument is an integer, then the return value is just the argument. If the argument is not an integer, then ceil() returns the next-larger integer while floor() returns the next-smaller integer. Note that "integer" here does not mean an int; it means a value with no fractional part.

A terse summary of the ceiling and floor methods is as follows: The ceiling of a number is the smallest integral double value that is not less than the number. The floor of a number is the largest integral double value that is not greater than the number.

Table 9.2 shows some examples of the values returned by the ceil() and floor() methods.

TABLE 9.2: Ceilings and Floors

x	ceil(x)	floor(x)
4	4	4
4.1	5	4
–4.1	–4	–5

The *max()* and *min()* Methods

The max() and min() methods both take two arguments. max() returns the larger of its arguments, while min() returns the smaller. These methods are overloaded: There are four versions of each.

The four max() methods are as follows:

- public int max(int a, int b)
- public long max(long a, long b)
- public float max(float a, float b)
- public double max(double a, double b)

The four min() methods are as follows:

- public int max(int a, int b)
- public long max(long a, long b)
- public float max(float a, float b)
- public double max(double a, double b)

The *random()* Method

The random() method returns a random double value. The return value is greater than or equal to zero, and strictly less than one.

The *round()* Method

The two round() methods are as follows:

- public int round(float f)
- public long round(double d)

The first version returns the int that is closest to the float argument. The second version returns the long that is closest to the double argument. The method rounds up if its argument falls exactly between two consecutive integers. Table 9.3 shows some examples of rounded values.

TABLE 9.3: Examples of Rounded Values

x	Math.round(x)
1.001	1
1.999	2
-1.001	-1
-1.999	-2
1.5	2
-1.5	-1

The *sin()*, *cos()*, and *tan()* Methods

The three trigonometric methods sin(), cos(), and tan() have double arguments and return types:

- public double sin(double angle)
- public double cos(double angle)
- public double tan(double angle)

The angle argument is always expressed in radians, not in degrees. The exam does not require you to know the technical definitions of sine, cosine, tangent, or radian.

The *sqrt()* Method

The sqrt() method has a double argument and return type. If the argument is greater than or equal to zero, then the return value is the square root of the argument. If the argument is less than zero, then the return value is Double.NaN, which connotes "Not a number." The sqrt() method never throws an exception, even if the argument is negative.

Standard IEEE 754 describes Double.NaN and similar pathological values and the proper behavior of these values under common arithmetic methods and operations. Fortunately, the details of IEEE 754 are beyond the scope of the Certification Exam.

Exam Essentials

Understand the **Math.abs()** method.   You should understand what the absolute value function does.

Understand the **ceil()** and **floor()** methods.   You should know that these methods have double return type, and return the next-larger and the next-smaller integral values, respectively.

Understand the **max()** and **min()** methods.   You should know that these methods each take two arguments, and return the maximum and the minimum of their arguments, respectively.

Understand the **random()** method.   You should know that the return value is greater than or equal to 0 and strictly less than 1.

Understand the **round()** method.   You should know that the method rounds up if its argument falls exactly between two consecutive integers.

Understand the **sin()**, **cos()**, and **tan()** methods.   You should know that the arguments to these methods are in radian units.

Understand the **sqrt()** method.   You should know that this method never throws an exception, even if the argument is negative.

Key Terms and Concepts

Absolute value   The absolute value of a non-negative number is the number itself. The absolute value of a negative number is the inverse of the number (thus, positive). An absolute value is always zero or positive.

Ceiling   The ceiling of a number is the smallest integral double value that is not less than the number.

Floor   The floor of a number is the largest integral double value that is not greater than the number.

Sample Questions

1. What does the following method print out?

```
System.out.println("abs(-1.5)=" + Math.abs(-1.5));
System.out.println("abs(0)=" + Math.abs(0));
System.out.println("abs(1.5)=" + Math.abs(1.5));
```

Answer: The code prints the following:

```
abs(-1.5)=1.5
abs(0)=0
abs(1.5)=1.5
```

The absolute value of a negative argument is the inverse of the argument. The absolute value of 0 is 0, and the absolute value of a positive argument is the argument itself.

2. What are the value and the type of Math.ceil(-1.1)?

Answer: The value is –1 and the type is double. The ceiling of an argument is the next-larger integral number, returned as a double.

3. What method of the `java.lang.Math` class returns the smaller of its two arguments?

Answer: `min()`. A similar method, `max()`, returns the greater of its two arguments.

4. In the code fragment below, can you guarantee that line 4 will never execute? Can you guarantee that line 6 will never execute?

```
1. while (true) {
2.    double d = Math.random();
3.    if (d == 0)
4.      System.out.println("d is zero");
5.    if (d == 1)
6.      System.out.println("d is one");
7. }
```

Answer: No, and yes. The `random()` method returns a value that is greater than or equal to zero, so you cannot guarantee that line 4 will never execute, despite the appalling odds. The return value is always less than one, so you can guarantee that line 6 will never execute.

5. What is `Math.round(-99.5)`?

Answer: –99. The `round()` method rounds up if its argument's fractional part is .59.

6. What are the units of the argument of the `Math.tan()` method?

Answer: Radians. All of Java's trigonometric methods use radians, not degrees.

7. In the code fragment below, does line 5 execute?

```
1. try {
2.    double d = Math.sqrt(-100);
3. }
4. catch (Exception e) {
5.    System.out.println("Oops");
6. }
```

Answer: No. The `Math.sqrt()` method never throws an exception, even when its argument is negative.

Describe the significance of the immutability of String objects.

This objective simply requires you to be aware that String objects are immutable. This immutability has several consequences.

Critical Information

An instance of the `java.lang.String` class encapsulates a run of 16-bit Unicode characters. How the class stores the characters is of course an implementation detail that programmers do not know and do not need to know.

Once an instance of `java.lang.String` is constructed, its contents are never changed. There are two situations in which the contents might *seem* to change:

- Calling one of the String's data modification methods
- Reassigning an instance variable of type `String`

These situations are reviewed in the following sections. We then examine the literal string pool, which can only usefully exist because strings are immutable.

Calling a Data Modification Method

The `String` class provides several methods whose names can be misleading if you are unfamiliar with the immutability of strings. For example, you might think that the `toUpper()` method, as called in the following code, modifies the contents of the current string, converting all lowercase characters to uppercase (see Figure 9.1).

```
1. String s = "aBcDe";
2. s.toUpper();
```

FIGURE 9.1: What toUpper() *doesn't* do

Original string object

The toUpper() call in line 2 above actually leaves the original string object alone (of course! String objects never change). The method call creates and returns a second instance of String. The second instance is very much like the original (all characters are simply uppercase), but there are two distinct objects. Figure 9.2 shows what the toUpper() method really does.

FIGURE 9.2: What toUpper() really does

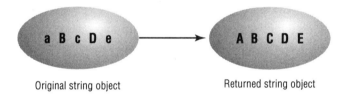

Original string object   Returned string object

Reassigning an Instance Variable of Type *String*

The following code fragment might be confusing:

```
1. String s = "Hello ";
2. s += "World";
```

The code might seem to modify the original string object at line 2. This is, of course, impossible, since strings are immutable. Line 2 constructs a second string object and reassigns s to reference the new object. (The original object becomes eligible for garbage collection.)

The Literal String Pool

A *literal string* is a string that is represented in source code by a run of text enclosed in double quotes. Line 1 below is an example of a literal string; line 2 is not.

```
1. "I have a double-quote fore and aft."
2. (new Integer(1234)).toString();
```

Every literal string is represented internally by an instance of java .lang.String. These strings are kept in a pool, created at compile time, that guarantees no duplication of literal strings. When a literal string is first compiled, the compiler adds a corresponding instance of String into the literal pool. If an identical literal string is encountered later during compilation, the compiler does not create a second instance of String; instead, the preexisting instance that was already in the pool is reused. Thus, no matter how many times a literal string appears in source code, only one String object is ever created, resulting in potentially significant memory savings.

The literal string pool concept works because strings are immutable. You don't mind sharing a literal string with another bit of code, as long as the other bit of code never surprises you by modifying the shared string.

The following code fragment illustrates one result of the literal string pool:

```
1. String s1 = "Abcde";
2. String s2 = "Abcde";
3. if (s1 == s2)
4.    System.out.println("Line 4 executes");
```

Line 4 executes because line 2 does not create a new instance of String; instead, the instance that was created in line 1 is reused.

Exam Essentials

Understand the immutability of the java.lang.String class. Be aware that the encapsulated characters are never modified under any circumstances. Realize that a method that appears to modify a string actually constructs and returns a different instance.

Be able to recognize a literal string. Understand the literal string pool. You should know how the literal pool enforces nonduplication of literal strings.

Key Terms and Concepts

Literal string A string that appears in source code as a run of text enclosed in double quotes. Literal strings are represented by instances of java.lang.String in the literal string pool.

Literal string pool A collection of strings that represent, without duplication, literal strings that appear in source.

Sample Questions

1. What does the following code fragment print?

```
1. String s1 = "ABC":
2. String s2 = s1;
3. s1 += "xyz";
4. System.out.println(s2);
```

Answer: The code prints out "ABC". Line 3 does not modify the original string; rather, it constructs and returns a new string object.

2. Does line 4 below execute?

```
1. String s1 = "ABC";
2. String s2 = "ABC";
3. if (s1 == s2)
4. System.out.println("Yes");
```

Answer: Yes. There is only one String object in lines 1 and 2. Since the literal strings are identical, they are represented by a single entry in the literal pool.

Chapter

10

The *java.util* Package

**SUN CERTIFIED PROGRAMMER FOR JAVA 2
PLATFORM EXAM OBJECTIVE COVERED IN
THIS CHAPTER:**

▶ Make appropriate selection of collection classes/
interfaces to suit specified behavior requirements.

This chapter covers a single objective. Collections were introduced in Java 2, and the exam requires you to have some familiarity with their use. Proper use of collections can greatly enhance program performance and maintainability.

Make appropriate selection of collection classes/interfaces to suit specified behavior requirements.

This objective deals with the Collections API, which was introduced in Java 2. The various classes of this API appear easy to use, but there are some subtleties to their use and behavior. A good understanding of collections is essential to effective Java programming. The presence of this objective reflects the importance of collections.

Critical Information

The *Collections API* consists of 23 interfaces and classes within the java.util package that define and implement behavior for organized data collections. This large number may appear intimidating, but for our purposes it is in fact good news, since it would be unreasonable to require you to have intimate working knowledge of all 23 interfaces and classes.

However, it is important for you to have a solid grasp of the big picture. In this section we will review the following important big-picture issues that relate to collections:

- The major interfaces: List, Set, and Map
- Thread safety

- Appropriate reference type

The Major Collections Interfaces

The three major interfaces of the Collections API are List, Set, and Map. List and Set extend the Collection superinterface; Map does not extend any superinterface. The hierarchy of these interfaces is shown in Figure 10.1.

FIGURE 10.1: Collections interface hierarchy

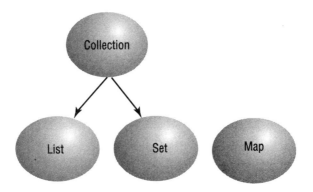

The methods of the Collection superinterface are listed as follows. It is worthwhile to read the method descriptions because some of the method behavior is unexpected. In general, methods that attempt to modify the collection, either by adding or removing items, return a boolean that states whether the collection was actually modified.

public boolean add(Object ob)   Ensures ob is in the current collection, adding ob if appropriate. Returns true if ob was added.

public boolean addAll(Collection c)   Ensures every element of c is in the current collection, adding elements of c if appropriate. Returns true if any elements were added.

public void clear()   Removes all elements from the current collection.

public boolean contains(Object ob)   Returns true if the current collection contains one or more elements equal to ob. The test for equality is the equals() method, not the == operator.

public boolean containsAll(Collection c)   Returns true if the current collection contains one or more elements equal to each element of c. The test for equality is the equals() method, not the == operator.

public boolean equals(Object ob)   Returns true if ob is equal to the current collection.

public int hashCode()   Returns a hash code for the current collection.

public boolean isEmpty()   Returns true if the collection does not contain any elements.

public Iterator iterator()   Returns an iterator over the current collection.

public boolean remove(Object ob)   If the current collection contains one or more elements equal to ob, then one of those elements is removed. The test for equality is the equals() method, not the == operator. Returns true if anything was removed.

public boolean removeAll(Collection c)   Removes from the current collection every element that is equal to an element of c. The test for equality is the equals() method, not the == operator. Returns true if anything was removed.

public boolean retainAll(Collection c)   Removes from the current collection every element that is not equal to an element of c. The test for equality is the equals() method, not the == operator. Returns true if anything was removed.

public int size()   Returns the number of elements in the current collection.

public Object[] toArray()   Returns an Object array that contains all the elements of the current collection.

public Object[] toArray(Object[] arr)   Returns an array that contains all the elements of the current collection. The class of the array is the same as the class of arr.

Many of the methods in this list rely on the equals() methods of the elements of the current collection. A "contract" governs the behavior of the equals() and hashCode() methods. It is described on the API page for the Object class. The contract states that given any two objects ob1 and ob2, ob1.equals(ob2) implies ob1.hashCode() == ob2.hashCode(). The collection classes expect their elements to honor this contract; the collection classes' own equals() and hashCode() methods honor the contract.

The *List* Interface

The List interface defines the behavior of a family of collection classes where the elements are arranged in linear order. If a list has *n* elements, then every element has a unique index from 0 through *n*–1. Lists are allowed to contain duplicate elements.

In addition to the methods inherited from the Collection superinterface, the List interface defines the following methods:

public void add(int index, Object ob)   Inserts ob at position index. The element originally at index, and all subsequent elements, are moved down to make room for the new element.

public void addAll(int index, Collection c)   Inserts all the elements of c at position index. The element originally at index, and all subsequent elements, are moved down to make room for the new elements.

public Object get(int index)   Returns the element at the specified position.

public Object indexOf(Object ob)   Returns the index of the first element in the current list that equals ob, or –1 if no matching element is found. The test for equality is the equals() method, not the == operator.

public Object lastIndexOf(Object ob)   Returns the index of the last element in the current list that equals ob, or –1 if no matching element is found. The test for equality is the equals() method, not the == operator.

public ListIterator listIterator()   Returns a list iterator over the current list. A list iterator supports bidirectional list traversal and is capable of modifying the list.

public ListIterator listIterator(int index) Returns a list iterator over the subset of the current list that begins at index.

public Object remove(int index) Removes and returns the element at index.

public Object set(int index, Object ob) Replaces the element at index with ob. Returns the object that was originally at index.

public List subList(int fromIndex, int toIndex) Returns a subset of the current list. The returned list is a "view" into the current list, in the sense that changes to the current list are reflected in the returned list, and vice versa.

The List interface is implemented by the abstract AbstractList class, which has four non-abstract subclasses, as shown in Figure 10.2.

FIGURE 10.2: The List hierarchy

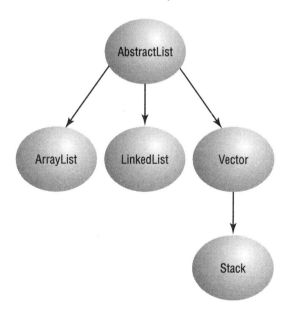

The four non-abstract list classes offer the following functionality:

ArrayList   An implementation that uses an array for internal storage.

LinkedList   An implementation that uses a linked list for internal storage.

Vector   One of the original Java data storage classes, predating the Collections API. Unlike most other collection classes, this class is synchronized. (See the "Thread Safety" section later in this chapter for a discussion of collections and synchronization issues.)

Stack   A subclass of **Vector** that supports stack operations such as pushing and popping. Unlike most other collection classes, this class is synchronized.

The *Set* Interface

The **Set** interface defines a family of collection classes that contain no duplicate elements. As usual, the test for duplication is the **equals()** method rather than the == operator. **Set** does not define any methods beyond those inherited from the **Collection** superinterface.

If s1 and s2 are sets, then s1.addAll(s2) produces the union of the two sets, while s1.retainAll(s2) produces the intersection of the two sets.

The *Map* Interface

The **Map** interface, unlike **List** and **Set**, does not extend the **Collection** superinterface. The **Map** interface defines a family of collection classes that map keys to values. There are generally no restrictions on the class of a key or the class of a value. Each key corresponds to a single value. A map may not contain duplicate keys (though duplicate values are permitted). The test for duplication is the **equals()** method rather than the == operator.

The methods of the **Map** interface are listed below. Note that since maps contain key/value pairs, we refer to the *mappings* of a map, rather than its elements. A mapping is a key/value pair.

public void clear()   Removes all mappings from the current map.

public boolean containsKey(Object key) Returns true if the current map contains a mapping whose key is equal to key. The test for duplication is the equals() method rather than the == operator.

public boolean containsValue(Object value) Returns true if the current map contains at least one mapping whose value is equal to value. The test for duplication is the equals() method rather than the == operator.

public Set entrySet() Returns a set that contains the mappings of the current map. The elements of the return-value set are instances of the Map.Entry interface, which is an inner interface within the Map interface. A Map.Entry has methods that return the corresponding entry's key and value.

public boolean equals(Object ob) Returns true if ob is equal to the current collection.

public Object get(Object key) Returns the value associated with key. Returns null if the current map does not contain a mapping for key.

public int hashCode() Returns a hash code for the current map.

public boolean isEmpty() Returns true if the current map does not contain any mappings.

public Object put(Object key, Object value) Adds to the current map a mapping association between key and value. If the current map previously contained a mapping for key, returns the old value associated with key; returns null if there was no previous mapping for key.

public void putAll(Map m) Adds all mappings from m to the current map. If the current map previously contained mappings for keys that appear in m, those old mappings are replaced with the mappings from m.

public Object remove(Object key) Removes the mapping for key from the current map, if one is present. Returns the value originally associated with key if one existed, or null if there was no such mapping.

public int size()   Removes the number of mappings in the current map.

public Collection values()   Returns a collection containing all the values of the current map. Changes to the map are reflected in the returned collection, and vice versa.

Thread Safety

A class is *threadsafe* if any thread may call any method of any instance of the class at any time. The classes of the Collections API are generally not threadsafe. You should assume that a Collections class is not threadsafe unless its documentation explicitly states otherwise.

For example, consider the TreeMap class. If you read the Javadoc API page for this class, you find nothing in the class description to indicate that the class is threadsafe. (In fact, a paragraph explicitly says the class is *not* synchronized and explains how to deal with this situation.) If an instance of TreeMap is to be accessed concurrently by multiple threads that change the structure of the data collection, you will have to take your own measures, perhaps synchronizing the methods that access and modify the map, and choosing an appropriate object lock on which to synchronize. (Chapter 7, "Threads," reviews thread concurrency and synchronization.)

Appropriate Reference Type

The various classes that implement the List, Map, and Set interfaces are easily interchangeable if used correctly. It is important wherever possible to refer to collection instances with reference variables of interface type rather than of class type and to only call those methods that appear in the interface definition.

For example, consider a program that is developed around an instance of TreeMap, which implements the Map interface. Suppose the program has half a dozen methods that process the map's data in various ways. There are two ways to declare the processing methods.

The methods might be declared to take a TreeMap argument, as follows:

```
void method1(TreeMap tm) { ... }
```

```
void method2(TreeMap tm) { ... }
void method3(TreeMap tm) { ... }
void method4(TreeMap tm) { ... }
void method5(TreeMap tm) { ... }
void method6(TreeMap tm) { ... }
```

Creation and processing of the map might look like this:

```
1. TreeMap theMap = new TreeMap();
2. method1(theMap);
3. method2(theMap);
4. method3(theMap);
5. method4(theMap);
6. method5(theMap);
7. method6(theMap);
```

Now, suppose that at some point in the development cycle it becomes clear that the TreeMap implementation is not appropriate for the job at hand, and a HashMap would provide significantly better performance. All six of the map-processing method declarations now have to be modified, a tedious and error-prone chore. (For a real-world large-scale program, there are likely to be myriad more methods to find and modify.) Moreover, a different constructor has to be called, so line 1 above changes to

```
1. HashMap theMap = new HashMap();
```

This example shows the maintenance cost of using class-type references. It would be a much better strategy to declare all the methods to take arguments of type Map, as follows:

```
void method1(Map m) { ... }
void method2(Map m) { ... }
void method3(Map m) { ... }
void method4(Map m) { ... }
void method5(Map m) { ... }
void method6(Map m) { ... }
```

Similarly, there is a maintenance advantage to having *every* reference to the map be of type Map, rather than any particular implementing class. Thus the constructor line becomes

```
1. Map theMap = new HashMap();
```

Now the program can be converted from using a tree map to using a hash map, simply by changing the constructor call.

The exam tests you on your understanding of the advantage of referencing collections with interface-type references.

Exam Essentials

Be able to identify the major interfaces of the Collections API: List, Set, and Map.   You should be aware that these are interfaces, not classes, and that List and Set extend Collection.

Know the main characteristics of each kind of Collections API: List, Set, and Map.   Be aware that List maintains order, Set prohibits duplicate members, and Map associates keys with values.

Understand how collections test for duplication and equality.   Collections use the equals method rather than the == operator.

Understand that collection classes are not threadsafe.   Most implementation classes are not threadsafe. You should assume that a collection class is not threadsafe unless its API documentation explicitly states otherwise.

Understand why it is preferable for references to collections to have interface type rather than class type.   Be aware of the maintenance benefits when substituting one implementing class for another.

Key Terms and Concepts

Collections API   Twenty-three interfaces and classes in the java.util package that support organized collections of objects.

Equality The Collections API tests for equality using the equals() method, rather than the == operator.

List A collection that maintains linear order. List behavior is described by the List interface, which extends the Collection super-interface.

Map A collection that contains key/value mappings. Keys must be unique. Map behavior is described by the Map interface, which does not extend the Collection superinterface.

Mapping An association between a key and a value.

Set An unordered collection that does not permit duplicate elements. Set behavior is described by the Set interface, which extends the Collection superinterface.

Threadsafe A class is threadsafe if any thread may call any method of any instance of the class at any time.

Sample Questions

1. At the top of the next page is the name of the current chapter. Cover it with your hand. What package contains the interfaces and classes of the Collections API?

   Answer: java.util. All Collections interfaces and classes reside in the java.util package.

2. One of the four main interfaces of the Collections API is Collection. What are the other three interfaces?

   Answer: List, Map, and Set.

3. You want to construct an instance of class ArrayList. The class extends the List interface. Which of the following approaches is preferable?

   A. ArrayList myList = new ArrayList();

   B. List myList = new ArrayList();

Answer: B. Whenever possible, references to collections should have interface type rather than class type.

4. The application listed below constructs a set and calls the set's add() method three times. What value is printed out at line 10?

```java
public class A {
    public int hashCode() {return 1;}
    public boolean equals(Object b) {return true;}

    public static void main(String[] args) {
        Set set = new Hashset();
        set.add(new A());
        set.add(new A());
        set.add(new A());
        System.out.println(set.size());
    }
}
```

A. 0

B. 1

C. 3

D. Some value other than 0, 1, or 3

Answer: B. The code prints out "1". Even though the add() method is called three times, the second two calls are unsuccessful because sets do not allow duplication. All instances of class A are considered duplicates of one another, because all instances return the same hash code and all calls to equals() return true.

Chapter

11

The *java.io* Package

SUN CERTIFIED PROGRAMMER FOR THE JAVA 2 PLATFORM EXAM OBJECTIVES COVERED IN THIS CHAPTER:

- Write code that uses objects of the *File* class to navigate a file system.

- Write code that uses objects of the classes *InputStreamReader* and *OutputStreamWriter* to translate between Unicode and either platform default or ISO 8859-1 character encodings, and distinguish between conditions under which platform default encoding conversion should be used and conditions under which a specific conversion should be used.

- Select valid constructor arguments for *FilterInputStream* and *FilterOutputStream* subclasses from a list of classes in the *java.io.package*.

- Write appropriate code to read, write, and update files using *FileInputStream, FileOutputStream,* and *RandomAccessFile* objects.

- Describe the permanent effects on the file system of constructing and using *FileInputStream, FileOutputStream,* and *RandomAccessFile* objects.

You should be conversant with the basic capabilities of Java's file and file-system handling. Even programs that do not store information in persistent storage might need to read configuration information from a file. Since Java runs on multiple platforms, it is important that you comprehend the mechanisms that permit platform-independent navigation of file systems and that permit the reading and writing of data, even if the encoding used is not plain ASCII or does not match the platform's own conventions.

Write code that uses objects of the *File* class to navigate a file system.

This objective ensures that you know how to write code that navigates a file system without regard to the underlying platform conventions.

Critical Information

The File class provides several methods for navigating a file system. It is important to know the methods that allow you to do this and how to use them in a platform-independent way. These are the methods you should understand:

- String getParent()
- File getParentFile()
- File getAbsoluteFile
- String getAbsolutePath()
- String getPath()
- boolean isDirectory()

- `String[] list()`
- `File[] listFiles()`
- `static File[] listRoots()`

Given any `File` object, you can use the methods `getParent()` or `getParentFile()` to navigate up the directory hierarchy toward the root. Alternatively, you can start from each root in turn using the `listRoots()` method. Use the `listFiles()` method to determine the contents of each root, then the `isDirectory()` method to locate the directories, and proceed in this fashion down each directory as needed.

When navigating file systems, you should avoid creating string path names as a starting point. While this is acceptable when the user provides the information, since presumably the user is familiar with the file system conventions, it is awkward for a program to do this because of the variety of path specification formats. Because of this, it is generally better to use the navigation tools of the `File` class.

Exam Essentials

Know the methods of the `File` class that provide navigation tools and circumvent the need for constructing platform-specific path strings.   These methods are as follows: `getParent()`, `getParentFile()`, `getAbsoluteFile()`, `getAbsolutePath()`, `getPath()`, `isDirectory()`, `list()`, `listFiles()`, and `listRoots()`.

Key Term and Concept

Platform-independent file system navigation   Modern file systems can be represented as a hierarchical arrangement of files and directories based on one or more roots. However, the formats used to represent particular files in particular directories vary widely. Platform-independent file system navigation describes moving around in a file system without specific knowledge of how the paths are constructed, and is made possible by the abstractions in Java's File class.

Sample Questions

1. Given a File object representing the absolute path to a file called x.txt in a directory three levels from the root directory, which of these methods would be needed to create another File object that refers to a file called y.txt in the directory one level up from x.txt?

   A. getParentFile()

   B. getAbsoluteFile()

   C. isDirectory()

   D. listFiles()

   E. listRoots()

   F. File(File, String) // constructor

   Answer: A, F. If the variable fileX is a File object that refers to the file x.txt in the question, then the required effect would be obtained by the code: new File(fileX.getParentFile(), "y.txt").

2. Given a File object that represents the absolute path to a file called x.txt, which of these methods would be needed to create a list of all the directories in the same directory as x.txt?

   A. getParentFile()

   B. getAbsoluteFile()

   C. isDirectory()

   D. listFiles()

   E. listRoots()

   F. File(File, String) // constructor

Answer: A, C, D. The method getParentFile() provides a File object that represents the directory containing x.txt. Invoking the listFiles() method on that will give an array of File objects representing all the files and directories that are siblings with x.txt. Finally, a loop would be needed to select only the directories, the distinction being made by the method isDirectory().

Write code that uses objects of the classes *InputStreamReader* and *OutputStream-Writer* to translate between Unicode and either platform default or ISO 8859-1 character encodings, and distinguish between conditions under which platform default encoding conversion should be used and conditions under which a specific conversion should be used.

Multinational operations, for example, those with Web sites that provide customer access to the business, frequently need to handle a variety of languages from a single program. This objective is intended to ensure that you can write code that runs properly even when faced with the need to handle text in more than just one language.

Critical Information

Most platforms use an 8-bit character encoding convention that is specific to the part of the world in which they are used. Internally, Java uses Unicode characters to represent text. Unicode is a 16-bit character set that covers a large number of international languages. When text is transferred between the host environment and the Java Virtual Machine (JVM), appropriate translation is necessary.

The Java APIs provide two categories of mechanism for processing text. Streams are 8 bits wide and handle characters that are encoded in some nationality-specific way. Readers and Writers, on the other hand, are 16 bits wide and handle Unicode characters. `InputStreamReader` and `OutputStreamWriter` are two classes that provide for conversion between 8-bit and Unicode formats.

To read data from an 8-bit stream encoded in the local platform convention, simply construct an `InputStreamReader` with a single `InputStream` argument. The `InputStream` argument should be the object from which the 8-bit data is to be read. Conversely, to convert Unicode characters into 8-bit platform format, construct an `OutputStreamWriter` using the target `OutputStream` object as the sole argument.

Sometimes you may need to read or write an 8-bit format that is not appropriate to the host system's locale. This most often happens when working over a network, for example, with an Internet standard protocol such as FTP or SMTP. In many cases, the 8-bit format in these situations will be ASCII, regardless of the host system's locale. However, there are situations where it might be any other format.

To read or write a specific format, construct an `InputStreamReader` or `OutputStreamWriter`, as appropriate, but provide two arguments. The first is the target stream, as before. The second is the name of the specific encoding standard to be used by the 8-bit stream. For example, to read ASCII characters from the standard input channel, construct a reader like this:

```
new InputStreamReader(System.in, "8859_1")
```

A list of all supported platform-specific encoding formats is provided in the JDK tools documentation for the `native2ascii` program.

Exam Essentials

Understand the relationship between platform encoding standards, Unicode, Streams, Readers, Writers, and the Unicode standard used in the JVM. Underlying platforms generally use 8-bit formats for keyboard, screen, and file IO. This is most closely represented by Streams. By contrast, Readers and Writers use 16-bit Unicode. Unicode is also used in the JVM, so it makes sense that the JVM should read from Readers and write to Writers.

Know how to use `InputStreamReader` and `OutputStreamWriter` to convert between Unicode and nation-specific encoding formats. To convert between 8-bit formats and Unicode, use the `InputStreamReader` and `OutputStreamWriter` classes. `InputStreamReaders` and `OutputStreamWriters`, if created with only one argument, convert between the host platform's encoding format, specified by the host system's locale, and Unicode. A second argument to the constructor of `InputStreamReader` or `OutputStreamWriter` causes them to convert between Unicode and an explicitly named encoding format (named by the second argument).

Key Terms and Concepts

Character encoding A mapping between a small number (typically 8- or 16-bits wide) and a set of characters that may be used to represent text in some language or languages.

Locale The set of language, character set, and other conventions (such as currency and date presentation format) that are appropriate to a given geographical or cultural preference.

Reader A 16-bit-wide data pipe from which Unicode text may be read.

Stream An 8-bit-wide data pipe. An `InputStream` is a stream from which bytes may be read, and an `OutputStream` is one into which bytes may be written.

Unicode A 16-bit-wide character encoding standard. Unicode is used by all Java Virtual Machines (except Micro Edition, which is not covered by the exam) for representing text. It represents most characters in most modern languages.

Writer A 16-bit-wide pipe into which Unicode text may be written.

Sample Questions

1. Which would be suitable for reading text from a file "`text.txt`", where the file is supplied from a U.S.-based company but the program might be running in any locale anywhere in the world?

A. new `FileInputStream("text.txt")`

B. new `File("text.txt")`

C. new `InputStreamReader("text.txt")`

D. new `InputStreamReader(`
new `FileInputStream("text.txt"))`

E. new `InputStreamReader(`
new `FileInputStream("text.txt"), "8859_1")`

Answer: E. This form uses the `FileInputStream` object to read the raw data from the file and constructs the `InputStreamReader`, configured to translate from ISO 8859-1 format into Unicode. ISO 8859-1 is equivalent to ASCII.

2. Which would be suitable for reading text from a file "`text.txt`", where the file was created by the reading system or another in the same office?

A. new `FileInputStream("text.txt")`

B. new `File("text.txt")`

C. new `InputStreamReader("text.txt")`

D. new `InputStreamReader(`
new `FileInputStream("text.txt"))`

E. new InputStreamReader(
    new FileInputStream("text.txt"), "8859_1")

Answer: D. This form uses the default conversion as appropriate to the locale configured for the host platform.

Select valid constructor arguments for *FilterInputStream* and *FilterOutput-Stream* subclasses from a list of classes in the *java.io.package*.

This objective is intended to ensure you have a clear grasp of the way filter streams can be plugged together to provide complex filtering out of several simple filters.

Critical Information

This one is easy. FilterInputStream subclasses need an InputStream object as the constructor argument, while FilterOutputStream subclasses need an OutputStream argument. Because FilterInputStream is a subclass of InputStream, and FilterOutputStream is a subclass of OutputStream, it is entirely valid (and common) to use a filter stream as a constructor argument to another stream. The only provision is that the streams must be of the same "direction," meaning that input streams do not mix with output streams.

FilterInputStream classes generally have names that make the fact that they are filters fairly clear. These are the main filter input streams in JDK 1.2:

- BufferedInputStream
- CheckedInputStream
- DataInputStream
- DigestInputStream

- `InflaterInputStream`
- `LineNumberInputStream`
- `ProgressMonitorInputStream`
- `PushbackInputStream`

The main filter output streams in JDK 1.2 are as follows:

- `BufferedOutputStream`
- `CheckedOutputStream`
- `DataOutputStream`
- `DeflaterOutputStream`
- `DigestOutputStream`
- `PrintStream`

You probably do not need to learn these stream names; it is sufficient to recognize them as filter streams if you see them. Notice how the names (with the exception of `PrintStream`) describe behavior. Streams that are not filters tend to describe the end point of the data they operate with, for example, `FileOutputStream` or `ByteArrayInputStream`.

Exam Essentials

Know that `FilterInputStream` classes need an `InputStream` object as a constructor argument, while `FilterOutputStream` classes need an `OutputStream` object as a constructor argument. Since filter streams are subclasses of the basic streams, filters may be joined in sequences.

Key Term and Concept

Filter stream Either an input (`FilterInputStream`) or an output (`FilterOutputStream`) subclass. Filters provide additional functionality to a stream and behave as if "plugged into" the preexisting stream.

Sample Question

1. Which are syntactically valid arguments to the constructor of
BufferedInputStream?

A. BufferedInputStream

B. BufferedOutputStream

C. FileInputStream

D. FileOutputStream

E. File

Answer: A, C. File is not a stream, so E is wrong. The direction of
streams must match, so the output streams are inappropriate too.
Although it would be rather pointless, a BufferedInputStream is
valid, since it matches only one criterion: that the object should be
some subclass of InputStream. A FileInputStream also satisfies this
criterion and is actually a reasonable thing to do.

Write appropriate code to read, write and update files using *FileInputStream, FileOutputStream,* and *RandomAccessFile* objects.

This objective is intended to ensure you have a clear grasp of
basic file IO operations using these fundamental classes.

Critical Information

A FileInputStream object may be created using either a File or a
String to describe the actual file from which reading should occur.
The FileInputStream object never changes the target file and generally reads sequentially starting from the beginning, although it is possible to skip over bytes using the skip() method.

As with the `FileInputStream`, a `FileOutputStream` object may be created using either a `File` or a `String` to describe the actual file to which writing should occur. If the constructor that takes a second argument of type `boolean` is used, then a `FileOutputStream` can be constructed that appends data to the end of an existing file. The other constructors create a `FileOutputStream` and simultaneously erase any contents in the named file if it already exists. If the file does not exist, it is created.

A `RandomAccessFile` object supports reading and writing on the same object and allows seeking to arbitrary positions, so the file need not be accessed purely from beginning to end. The first argument to the constructors for `RandomAccessFile` is either a `File` or a `String`. The second argument is a `String` that describes if the file is to be used for read-only or read/write access. The string should be either "r" or "rw" to indicate these two options.

A variety of methods are provided for reading and writing a random access file with any of the primitive data types, or with `String`. In fact, `RandomAccessFile` implements both the `DataInput` and `DataOutput` interfaces.

Attempting to write to a random access file that has been opened for read-only access throws an exception.

Exam Essentials

Know how to read from a file using `FileInputStream`. Simply create the object with either a `File` or a `String` filename.

Know how to overwrite or append to a file using `FileOutputStream`. Constructed with a `boolean` argument, a `FileOutputStream` can append to a file. Otherwise, it sets the length to zero when the object is constructed, which effectively deletes any preexisting data in the file.

Know how to use a `RandomAccessFile` for reading and writing and how to seek to a given point in the file. Understand and recognize the methods defined in the `DataInput` and `DataOutput` interfaces.

Key Terms and Concepts

FileInputStream   Class that reads binary data from a file. Restricted to sequential read but able to skip over regions.

FileOutputStream   Class that writes binary data to a file. The object either overwrites a preexisting file entirely when it is constructed or appends to it. No seek or skip is possible.

RandomAccessFile   Class that can read and/or modify a file. This class can read and write any of the primitive types and can seek to arbitrary positions in the file.

Sample Questions

1. Which constructors create objects that can be used to append to an existing file?

   A. new File("file.dat")

   B. new FileInputStream("file.dat")

   C. new FileOutputStream("file.dat")

   D. new RandomAccessFile("file.dat")

   E. new DataOutputStream("file.dat")

   F. None of the above

   Answer: F. File objects describe files but do not access their contents. Input streams read but do not write data. The constructor in C would delete the original contents of the file, which doesn't fit the description of appending. The constructor in D is not valid, since it lacks the mode argument. Finally, DataOutputStream is a filter stream, requiring an output stream as the constructor argument, so the constructor as shown will not compile.

2. Which will read the 10th byte of the file "file.dat" into the variable c?

A. `FileInputStream in =`
`    new FileInputStream("file.dat");`
`in.skip(9);`
`int c = in.read();`

B. `FileInputStream in =`
`    new FileInputStream("file.dat");`
`in.skip(10);`
`int c = in.read();`

C. `FileInputStream in =`
`    new FileInputStream("file.dat");`
`int c = in.read(10);`

D. `RandomAccessFile raf =`
`    new RandomAccessFile("file.dat");`
`raf.seek(10);`
`int c = raf.readByte();`

Answer: A. B reads the 11th byte. C fails to compile as there is no read method that takes a numeric argument. D also fails to compile since the constructor requires a mode string as the second argument.

3. Which will modify only the 10th byte of the file "file.dat"?

A. `FileOutputStream out =`
`    new FileOutputStream("file.dat");`
`out.skip(9);`
`out.write('x');`

B. `FileOutputStream out = new`
`    FileOutputStream("file.dat", true);`
`out.skip(9);`
`out.write('x');`

C. `RandomAccessFile raf = new`
`    RandomAccessFile("file.dat", "rw");`
`raf.seek(9);`
`raf.writeChar('x');`

D. RandomAccessFile raf = new
    RandomAccessFile("file.dat", "rw");
    raf.seek(9);
    raf.write('x');

Answer: D. FileOuputStream does not provide a seek()
method. If constructed with a single argument, the whole file is
erased. If, instead, the constructor is called with a second argument of true, new data is appended to the file. C is wrong, since
the writeChar() method writes two bytes. The plain write()
method in D writes the low 8 bits.

Describe the permanent effects on the file system of constructing and using *FileInputStream*, *FileOutputStream*, and *RandomAccessFile* objects.

This objective is intended to ensure you understand the behavior of these fundamental classes in terms of the effect they have on the
host file system.

Critical Information

Constructing and using a FileInputStream has no effect on the host
file system beyond possibly updating the "last accessed" time stamp.
Since you cannot read this information from Java, this has no significant effect on the exam.

Constructing a FileOutputStream that represents a preexisting
file will delete the file's contents unless the constructor File-
OutputStream(String, boolean) is used and the boolean value
true is provided as the second argument. You should be fully
aware of this significant effect.

Constructing a RandomAccessFile never alters any preexisting file, but of course, subsequent operations on the RandomAccessFile object might. Writing to a FileOutputStream or RandomAccessFile object will add to or change the contents of the file as expected.

Data written to a file using a FileOutputStream are always written as bytes. By contrast, the RandomAccessFile object implements the methods of the DataOutput interface and writes primitive values and String objects. The sizes of primitive values in a file are the same as the apparent size in the JVM, which is 8 bits for byte and boolean, 16 bits for short and char, 32 bits for float and int, and 64 bits for double and long.

The RandomAccessFile object provides a seek(long) method. This method positions the file pointer at the specified position, measured in bytes from the start of the file. Seeking beyond the end of the file does not change the file, but a subsequent write will extend the file enough to fill the gap. The new data in the extended area is not defined. The method setLength() either truncates or extends the file immediately. Again, any new data at the end of the file are undefined.

Exam Essentials

Recognize which constructors will overwrite existing files, and which will not. FileInputStream and RandomAccessFile do not change any preexisting file when their constructors are invoked. FileOutputStream, however, can erase the contents of a file when it is constructed.

Know how the various write methods encode data when writing with either a FileOutputStream or a RandomAccessFile. FileOutputStream writes bytes, or arrays of bytes, only. The RandomAccessFile can write the primitive data types directly. This is done using the JVM's standard data format: 1 byte for byte and boolean, 2 bytes for char and short, 4 bytes for int and float, and 8 bytes for long and double.

Know how the **seek** method behaves when a **RandomAccessFile** seeks beyond the end of the file.   The file is not extended until the next write operation occurs.

Key Terms and Concepts

File extension   A file may be extended beyond its previous length, using the seek() or setLength() methods of the RandomAccessFile class. In this case, the data between the original end and the new end are not defined.

File truncation   A file may be set to zero length, in which case the data it previously contained are effectively lost. This happens if the FileOutputStream constructor is invoked with only one argument, or the second argument is false.

Primitive data size   Each primitive data item has a fixed size and format when written externally by a JVM. This ensures that it is possible to take data written by one JVM on one platform and read it correctly on any other JVM on any other platform.

Sample Questions

1. How long is "file.dat" after running this code, assuming that the file does not exist beforehand?

```
1.  RandomAccessFile raf = new
2.     RandomAccessFile("file.dat", "rw");
3.     raf.write('x');
4.     raf.writeChar('x');
5.     raf.close();
```

A. 2 bytes

B. 3 bytes

C. 4 bytes

D. 8 bytes

E. Undefined

Answer: B. The first write writes a single byte, while the second writes the 2-byte Unicode representation of "x".

2. How long is the file that results from running the following code, assuming the target file is 10 bytes long beforehand?

```
1. FileOutputStream fos = new
2.     FileOutputStream(args[0], true);
3.     fos.write('x');
4.     fos.writeChar('x');
5.     fos.close();
```

A. 10 bytes

B. 12 bytes

C. 13 bytes

D. 14 bytes

E. Undefined

Answer: E. File output streams do not have methods that write any data other than bytes. So writeChar() at line 4 does not compile.

Appendix

A

The Certification Initiative for Enterprise Development

The Sun Certified Programmer's Exam has been very well received, and has won industry-wide support based on the validity of both the objectives and the questions. Much of this support results directly from the fact that the test is hard, and as such proves something worthwhile about you when you hold the certification. This general recognition led to an appropriate desire on the part of other vendors to be part of the success and relevance of Java certification. In consequence, some major players set up an organization called jCert, with the goal of creating the "Certification Initiative for Enterprise Development." The initiative aims to provide a suite of certification options that are essentially comparable in difficulty and relevance, but that focus on particular vendor's tools at the appropriate points. The slogan "Certified Once, Valued Everywhere" is used by the jCert organization to convey the consistency of value.

The initiative is open to new members, but as of June 2000, the jCert organization consisted of Sun, iPlanet (the Sun/Netscape Alliance), IBM, Oracle, BEA Systems, Novell, Hewlett-Packard, and Sybase. At that time, most of the member companies had not finalized their examinations. Because of this, we can really only describe the structure of the initiative, and outline the broad intent of the participant companies. To help you get the general picture, we have listed the objectives for the core exams and for the vendor examinations from IBM, since that company seems to be furthest along the road and has offerings that appear to be stable. You should refer to the jCert Web site, and the Web sites of the individual participants, to get up-to-date details on the various vendors' examinations.

The jCert organization site acts as the home for the entire initiative. The site is located at http://www.jcert.org/ and includes descriptions of the initiative and links to the certification program information of the individual members of the group.

The Structure of the Initiative

The initiative is composed of three levels of examinations, some of which are specific to particular vendors, and others of which are common to the initiative as a whole. Each level constitutes a certification in its own right, so you can get the benefit of fulfilling part of the overall certification before you complete the whole thing.

You must take the three levels in order, but you may change vendors between the levels if that suits you. The Level I exam is always the "Programmer's" exam—that is, the standard Sun Microsystems certification that is the topic of this book. So, all the hard work and preparation you put into achieving your programmer's certification is of value regardless of where you choose to seek your next level of certification.

The second and third levels both consist of two exams each. In each case, one exam is common across the whole initiative and the other is vendor-specific. The name of the certification you receive reflects the vendor-specific examination you chose to take at that level. If, for example, you took one of the IBM exams at the second level, you could call yourself an "IBM Certified Solution Developer." At the third level, if you chose an iPlanet examination, you would become an "iPlanet Certified Enterprise Developer."

One important point is that the Sun Microsystems Developer and Architect certifications are not part of this initiative. Rather, the focus of these two programs is independent of both tool and vendor, so if you have no interest in proving skills with a particular vendor's products, these exams might be a better choice for you.

The Second-Level Exams

Since the first step on the road to jCert certification is always Sun Microsystems' "Programmer's" exam, we will not discuss that here. Instead, we will go right ahead and describe the basic format of the second-level, or "Certified Solution Developer," exams.

There are three main areas of coverage in the Level II exams. These are:

- Your ability to use JDBC to access and manipulate data

- Your ability to develop and deploy applications in a heterogeneous networked environment (such as the Internet)

- Your understanding of object-oriented principles, your ability to apply these principles, and your ability to work with JavaBeans components

You must take two exams to gain the second level of certification.

The Common Exam at Level II

The first of the exams is common to the initiative as a whole and is produced by IBM. This exam covers object-oriented analysis and design (OOAD) skills, rather than Java programming skills. You will also be expected to demonstrate proficiency in Unified Modeling Language (UML). The exam title is "Object-Oriented Analysis and Design with UML"; it has two identifying numbers: Test 486 or 1Z0-513. The detailed objectives listed for the exam are listed here in six categories.

Development Process

Apply iterative and incremental processes.

Schedule project activities based on use cases.

Exhibit the ability to trace requirements both forward and backward through OOAD artifacts.

Utilize use cases to drive other project activities.

Apply the appropriate OOAD activities for a given situation, based on their strengths and weaknesses.

Control and coordinate the interfaces between packages.

Organize the project team responsibilities based on OOAD artifacts.

Requirements Modeling

Identify skills and resources needed to write use cases.

Identify actors for the system.

Identify use cases from a requirement document and/or domain expert and extract business rules for the domain.

Develop and interpret a use case model using the UML notation.

Write use cases that focus on the problem domain.

Write use cases using the terminology of the target audience.

Derive subsequent OOAD artifacts from use cases.

Use a prototype of the user interface for customer feedback when appropriate.

Architecture

Develop view-model-persistence layered architectures and understand how the layers should interact.

Use package diagrams when appropriate, creating and interpreting contractual interfaces and dependencies between packages.

Use cohesion and coupling effectively when grouping classes into packages.

Use deployment diagrams effectively.

Apply brokering to build flexible systems.

Consider issues related to scalability, performance, transactions, and concurrency.

Static Modeling

Identify domain objects, services, attributes, and their relationships using different techniques, including "parts of speech."

Determine when a new class is needed.

Choose good names for classes and methods.

Describe the business concept and role that each class represents in the domain model.

Develop and interpret UML class diagrams, including the effective use of aggregation, generalization, and delegation.

Effectively interpret and develop associations in class diagrams, including stereotypes, qualified associations, cardinality of associations, and association classes.

Maintain encapsulation of attributes and visibility of operations effectively.

Recognize and exploit polymorphism.

Create, interpret, and exploit interfaces.

Interpret class diagrams from different perspectives, including subclassing and subtyping.

Create and interpret CRC cards as appropriate.

Dynamic Modeling

Focus on behavior while modeling the domain.

Include an appropriate level of detail in diagrams.

Effectively assign responsibilities to appropriate classes.

Develop UML interaction diagrams (sequence and collaboration) to satisfy requirements.

Interpret interaction diagrams, including the use of iterations, conditionals, and concurrency.

Recognize complexities early in the project and resolve them in an iterative and incremental fashion.

Determine when to use state diagrams.

Develop and interpret UML state diagrams, including the use of events, guards, actions, and super state.

Determine when to use activity diagrams.

Develop and interpret UML activity diagrams, including concurrency, iterations, and conditionals.

Design and Implementation Techniques

Design for reuse.

Given its definition, apply a pattern.

Refactor classes to distribute responsibilities and behavior.

Carry OOAD artifacts forward into implementation.

Resolve implementation issues and update OOAD artifacts

You will probably notice that some of these objectives are rather broad in scope. Of course, this is a rather different exam from the Programmer's test that you have probably spent much time studying for. Fortunately, IBM provides an online sample test that allows you to get a reasonable idea of the scope of the test. The pre-tests can be found by following the link at http://www.jcert.org/sponsors.html for IBM, which takes you to the IBM site that handles Java certification issues. The pre-test for test 486 can be found via the links for any of the "IBM Certified Solution Developer" tests. At the time of writing, this takes you to:

http://www-4.ibm.com/software/ad/certify/sam486a.html

TIP   One point about the IBM sample test site. You will be required to register before you can take the sample test. There's no cost involved, but they do give you a user id and password (which you can't control) and the password is splendidly secure—which means it's utterly impossible to remember; mine is poxp6cd7 (I'm not telling you my username ☺). Since the site doesn't seem to provide any means of recovering a forgotten password, you'll either have to re-register each time you use the site, or you really do need to make a note of the login information they provide.

The Vendor-Specific Exams at Level II

The second exam is the vendor-specific one, which will test core aspects of your skills in creating applications, but will also examine your ability to make efficient use of the vendor's tool while performing the programming work.

The vendor exams all cover comparable material, but of course since they deal with your ability to use the vendor's tool, there will be significant variations in the material. The general objectives for all vendor-specific Level II exams can be summarized as follows:

- Use the tool effectively for coding, testing, version control, and deployment, including appropriate use of JAR files and Beans components.

- Be able to create applications that use either JDBC or forms-based database access.

At the time of writing, you had a choice of three vendor-specific exams at Level II: two from IBM and one Oracle.

The IBM tests are numbered 282 and 494. Test 282 covers development with IBM VisualAge for Java, while test 494 covers IBM WebSphere Application Server, Standard Edition, V3. What follows are the objectives for these exams:

The IBM VisualAge for Java Exam

The IBM exam number 282 covers IBM VisualAge for Java. These are its objectives:

Construct and Deploy Java-Based Solutions, Including Applications, Applets, and Servlets

For a given situation, choose the appropriate type of Java program (Application, Applet, or Servlet) and assess their basic technical requirements.

Deploy Java code and associated files for Applets, Servlets, and Applications.

Access Databases and Use Remote Method Invocation (RMI) in the Development of Java-Based Solutions

Access databases using Data Access Beans, JDBC, SQLJ.

Connect database query results to forms or UI controls.

Use VisualAge for Java to aid implementation of RMI.

Use Visual Programming and the Existing Library of JavaBeans to Create Java-Based Solutions

Add JavaBeans to the Composition Surface.

Create connections in the Composition Editor and recognize meaning of the different types and appearances of connections.

Change the properties and parameters of connections.

Explain how and when to promote Bean features.

Modify Bean settings and understand the resulting changes that occur on the composition surface and in generated code.

Reorder connections and understand the effects.

Tear off properties of a JavaBean and understand the resulting changes that occur on the composition surface and in generated code.

Use Variables on the Composition Surface and understand the results on the composition surface and in the generated code.

Use and modify Visual Beans.

Use the Morph Into function on the Composition Editor.

Apply appropriate Bean given a required functionality (such as, use proper Visual Bean for required user interface).

Use the Visual Composition Editor to specify, change, and configure the layout and layout manager of a Visual Bean.

Identify and change the tab order of Visual Beans.

Create or consume re-usable panels (i.e., forms).

Use Object Factories and understand the results on composition surface and generated code.

Understand how and when to use the Beans List.

Create and use Quick Forms.

Create Re-Usable JavaBeans Using VisualAge for Java

Use the BeanInfo Page to create and modify JavaBean features (properties, events, methods) and be aware of what code is generated in the class and its corresponding BeanInfo class.

From the BeanInfo Page, create new Event Sets and Listeners, know what methods are generated, and be able to make use of them.

Create Property features using the various attributes a property can have (e.g., bound, constrained, expert, etc.) and be able to make use of them.

Set and use Property Editors and Bean Customizers.

Develop Java-Based Solutions Using VisualAge for Java

Write and modify Java code using the editors and editing aids provided by the IDE.

Understand the purpose of various Smartguides and be able to make use of them.

Make use of IDE features which aid Internationalization.

Import and export source code, resources, class files, and repository files.

Execute and test Applets, Applications, and Servlets from within the VisualAge for Java Environment.

Set the classpath in VisualAge for Java with each of the available techniques and explain the advantages and disadvantages of each technique.

Use the debugger to set and modify breakpoints, step through code, inspect variables, change the value of variables, etc.

Use the WebSphere Test Environment, Servlet Launcher, and JSP Monitor to execute and test servlets and JSPs.

Create Packages, Projects, Classes, Interfaces, methods, and fields.

Identify and resolve Java code errors, using facilities of the IDE.

Use the Code Management Facilities of VisualAge for Java

Access and manage repositories.

Implement version control for the different types of program elements, and use the 'compare' and 'replace with' functions of the IDE.

Understand the difference between the repository and the workspace.

Use Features of VisualAge for Java to Improve Development Productivity

Use and understand purpose of Console Window.

Identify and distinguish visual cues and clues.

Use the IDE's browsers to navigate and find information by making use of the features of the IDE such as bookmarks and search functions, as well as the different pages of each of the browsers.

Change the properties of browsers to display desired information.

Change and save the properties, settings, and options associated with the workspace.

Use the Quick Start Window.

The IBM WebSphere Application Server Exam

The IBM exam number 494 covers the WebSphere Application Server, Standard Edition. These are its objectives:

Overall Application Design

Determines the mechanism for managing client-specific state (e.g., Cookies, URL rewriting, hidden tags, HTTP sessions, etc.).

Designs a layered solution from a given multi-tiered architecture.

Designs and develops a solution to manage the decoupling of model from presentation.

Designs and develops model persistence using JDBC.

Controller Development

Designs and develops Java Servlets conforming to the JSDK 2.1 or JSWDK 1.X Specification.

Builds threadsafe, multi-user server-side programs.

Uses HttpSession objects to manage client-specific data on the server.

Knows when and how to use Cookies appropriately.

Knows when and how to use Security APIs appropriately.

Writes code to handle error conditions.

Builds and uses Java components to communicate between application layers (e.g., JavaBeans).

Examines HttpServletRequest objects in order to process client requests.

Sets properties of the HttpServletResponse and HttpServletRequest objects for controlling presentation content and application behavior.

Presentation Development

Modifies/constructs Web pages, to provide dynamic content using JSP.

Understands the JSP 1.0 Specification.

Configuration/Deployment

Knows IBM WebSphere Application Server architecture and terminology (e.g., startup sequence, plug-in, admin server, managed servers, property storage, etc.).

Installs and configures the IBM WebSphere Application Server.

Defines and/or configures Application Servers, Virtual Hosts, Web Applications, Web Resources, load-by-classname (invoker servlet), file server servlet, JDBC drivers, JSP enablers, Datasources, named servlets, Servlet Engines, and Web Paths.

Configures Session Manager options.

Uses Tasks, Types, and Topology configuration pages in the Administrative Console.

Starts, stops, and restarts Application Servers, Web Applications, and Servlet Engines.

Troubleshooting

Directs application and AdminServer trace outputs.

Interprets trace and log files to locate and solve problems.

Familiarity with tracing and debugging facilities.

Identifies and resolves concurrent programming issues.

Identifies misbehaving servlets and JSPs.

Identifies performance tuning opportunities.

Other Vendor Exams at Level II

At the time of writing, the only other jCert participant to offer reasonably stable information about a second-level test was Oracle. Their Level II test was actually available in two forms, one being phased out by the other, which was in beta test. Oracle's tests are based on the JDeveloper product, and the tests were being upgraded from Release 2 to account for Release 3. The codes for these versions are 1Z0-502 and 1Z1-512, respectively.

The Third-Level Exams

To achieve the designation "Certified Enterprise Developer," you must complete the third level of examinations, in addition to the first two. As with Level II, you must pass one common exam and one vendor-specific one. In this case, the common exam is owned by the jCert group, rather than by IBM.

The Common Exam at Level III

The Level III common exam covers the following broad areas:

- J2EE functional areas (the APIs)

- Security

- Enterprise JavaBean construction and deployment

- The EJB model (security, transactions, and so forth)

Although this exam is essentially a product of the jCert initiative, the details of the exam are not available from the jcert.org Web site. Instead, you can find this information at the IBM site, under IBM exam number 483. The test is called "Enterprise Connectivity Test with Java 2 Enterprise Edition." As with the other exams, IBM provides a sample test that will give you a feel for the type and difficulty of the questions. The objectives for this exam are divided into these six areas:

Java 2 Enterprise Edition (J2EE) Architecture

Select and apply appropriate J2EE technologies to design the desired multi-tiered architecture.

Evaluate tradeoffs in designing distributed systems.

Use given design patterns to encapsulate enterprise services in a multi-tiered application.

Assign responsibility to appropriate layers to optimize maintainability, scalability, and performance.

Web Component Development

Construct Web pages to provide dynamic content using JavaServer Pages (JSPs).

Design and develop Java Servlets conforming to the Java Servlet Specification, including Servlet life cycle, classes, and interfaces.

Coordinate and manage session state, including cookies, HttpSession, and URL rewrite.

Implement threadsafe server-side logic.

Implement robust controller logic within a framework which supports effective error handling.

Separate responsibilities between Servlets, Enterprise JavaBeans (EJBs), and JSPs.

Enterprise JavaBean (EJB) Development

Select and understand types of EJBs.

Design EJB home and remote interfaces.

Design logic compatible with EJB lifecycle and state behavior, including creation, activation, passivation, and removal.

Develop Entity EJBs with container-managed persistence (CMP) or bean-managed persistence (BMP).

Understand exceptions in the context of distributed objects and container-managed transactions.

Develop EJBs with bean-managed transactions, including UserTransaction and session synchronization.

Client Development

Customize payment processing.

Understand the issues of client-side programming, including application, servlet, and EJB clients.

Use Java Naming and Directory Interface (JNDI) to obtain references to services and publish available resources.

Use the UserTransaction type in a client application.

Connectivity Services

Select and use alternative distribution technologies, including remote method invocation (RMI), Java Messaging Service (JMS), and common object request broker architecture (CORBA).

Understand RMI issues for J2EE application design, including serialization, RMI-IIOP, and RemoteException.

Use JDBC 2.0 to access relational databases, including driver and statement selection.

Understand implications of JDBC 2.0 standard extension features on application design, including DataSources, connection pooling, and transaction management.

Assembly and Deployment

Package EJBs for portable deployment.

Understand content of the deployment descriptor and identify which architecture roles use which sections.

Assemble EJBs for deployment, including transaction demarcation and isolation level.

Establish security in a J2EE application.

The Vendor-Specific Exams at Level III

As with the Level II certification, the second exam at Level III is vendor-specific and relates to the use of the vendor's tools in complex development scenarios. Generally, the objectives of these exams will cover the following areas:

- Development of client and server components of an application using the tools and the following technologies and APIs: EJB, JSP and servlets, JDBC, connection pooling, transactions, and security.

- Test and deploy the application using the tools. Monitor and administer the application for best performance and reliability using the tools.

At the time of writing, exams or preliminary information were available for three vendor-specific exams at Level II, one each from IBM, Oracle, and iPlanet. Novell also offers the IBM exam under its own banner.

The IBM Vendor-Specific Exam

The IBM test is number 495, covering development with IBM WebSphere Application Server, Advanced Edition, V3. These are the objectives for this exam:

Application/Component Design

Designs and develops a solution that decouples model from presentation.

Identifies appropriate Enterprise JavaBean (EJB) type to solve a given business problem.

Uses appropriate design patterns to encapsulate services in an EJB application.

Web Component Development and Testing

Designs and develops Java Servlets conforming to the JSDK 2.1 Specification.

Builds and tests server-side logic which is threadsafe in a concurrent web application environment.

Manages end-user state using HttpSessions and cookies.

Implements robust controller logic within a framework which supports effective error handling.

Uses methods of HttpServletRequest and HttpServletResponse to interact with HTTP data streams.

Modifies/constructs Web pages to provide dynamic content using JSP 1.0.

Enterprise JavaBean (EJB) Development and Testing

Implements stateful/stateless Session Beans.

Implements container-managed persistence (CMP) Entity Beans.

Implements bean-managed persistence (BMP) Entity Beans.

Uses EJBContext to coordinate with the EJB container.

Uses client proxy to interface with EJBs.

Uses Java Transaction API (JTA) to control transaction demarcation.

Understands and works with Java Enterprise APIs to connect to EJBs.

Development and Testing of Applications with VisualAge for Java, Enterprise Edition, V3

Uses the WebSphere Test Environment to test Web applications within VisualAge for Java.

Uses VisualAge persistence to map CMP fields to existing database schemas.

Uses VisualAge EJB test client to unit test EJBs.

Uses EJB Development Environment in VisualAge for Java.

Selects and uses appropriate Access Bean(s) in order to provide client access to EJBs.

Configuration, Deployment, and Management of Applications

Manipulates transactional behavior of EJBs (e.g., isolation levels, transaction attribute).

Declares security policies on enterprise applications.

Uses WebSphere Administrative Console and related property files to configure and deploy an application.

Configures HttpSession management options.

Configures multi-node applications using Servlet Redirector and application server models/clones.

Uses the resource analyzer tool to identify performance tuning opportunities, connection pooling characteristics, etc.

Uses WebSphere trace facilities and log files to debug Application Server and Admin Server problems.

Identifies misbehaving servlets, JSPs, and EJBs.

Configures workload management selection policies.

Other Vendor Exams at Level III

Two other vendors had preliminary information about their exams at the time of writing; these are Oracle and iPlanet. The Oracle test is based on the Oracle Internet Platform product. The code for this exam is 1Z0-505, and it is called "Enterprise Development on the Oracle Internet Platform."

The iPlanet exam is called "iPlanet Application Server 6.0" and is identified as 310-540. If you take this route, you will be able to call yourself a "Sun/Netscape Alliance Certified Enterprise Developer."

Glossary

"Has a" "X has a Y" means that class X owns a variable of type Y.

"Is a" "X is a Y" means that class X extends class Y.

Absolute value The absolute value of a non-negative number is the number itself. The absolute value of a negative number is the inverse of the number (thus, positive). An absolute value is always zero or positive.

Abstract class An abstract class may not be instantiated.

Abstract method An abstract method contains no body, deferring definition to non-abstract subclasses.

Accessor A public method that returns private data.

Adapter In the AWT, the adapter classes are no-behavior implementations of some listener interfaces.

Application A Java class that contains a `public static void main(String[])` method, which can be invoked from the command line.

Argument list The command-line arguments passed into an application's main method.

Argument of a `switch` statement Must be `byte`, `short`, `char`, or `int`.

Argument of an `if` statement Must be `boolean`.

Arithmetic exception This exception type is only thrown on integer divide by zero or integer modulo zero.

Arithmetic promotion Conversion of an arithmetic operand to a wider type.

Array declaration The square brackets in the declaration can appear before or after the variable name.

Assignment promotion Conversion during assignment of a primitive or object reference to a compatible type.

Automatic variable A variable defined within the scope of a method.

BorderLayout The default layout manager for top-level containers (frame and dialog). The policy of this layout manager uses five regions and puts one component into each region.

Break Terminate execution of the current loop.

CardLayout This layout manager displays one component at a time in the full space of the container. Components can be selected for display one at a time from the full set of added components.

catch block A block of code that follows a `try` block and handles one specific exception type and its subclasses.

Ceiling The ceiling of a number is the smallest integral double value that is not less than the number.

Character encoding A mapping between a small number (typically 8 or 16 bits wide) and a set of characters that may be used to represent text in some language or languages.

Checked exception An exception type other than `RuntimeException` and its subclasses.

Collections API Twenty-three interfaces and classes in the `java.util` package that support organized collections of objects.

Component A parent class of all elements of a Java GUI.

Constraints object An object that describes how a component should be laid out. The object is passed with the component in the `add(Component, Object)` method of the `Container` class.

Container A subclass of component that is able to provide screen space to other components, including other containers.

Continue Terminate the current pass through the current loop.

Critical section A piece of code that could cause data corruption if another thread executes concurrently in the same context.

Deadlock A state where thread(s) are in a non-runnable state, waiting for a situation that is guaranteed not to occur because the thread is not running.

Deadly embrace The classic example of deadlock, in which two threads are waiting for resources, but each thread already holds the resource required by the other.

Default class A class with default access may be accessed by any class in the same package as the default class.

Default constructor A constructor with an empty argument list.

Default initialization values An array's elements are initialized to zero for numeric types and to values that resemble zero for non-numeric types.

Default inner class A default inner class may be accessed from the enclosing class and from subclasses of the enclosing class that reside in the same package as the enclosing class.

Default method A method with default access may be called by any class in the same package as the class that owns the default method.

Default variable A variable with default access may be read and written by any class in the same package as the class that owns the default variable.

Enclosing class A class that contains an inner class.

Enclosing method A method that contains an inner class.

Equality The Collections API tests for equality using the `equals()` method, rather than the `==` operator.

Event An object that carries information describing what happened when an event source calls a handler method in a listener.

Event source An object that can call handler methods in a listener to indicate that something of interest has occurred.

File extension A file may be extended beyond its previous length, using the `seek()` or `setLength()` methods of the `RandomAccessFile` class. In this case, the data between the original end and the new end are not defined.

File truncation A file may be set to zero length, in which case the data it previously contained are effectively lost. This happens if the `FileOutputStream` constructor is invoked with only one argument, or the second argument is `false`.

FileInputStream Class that reads binary data from a file. Restricted to sequential read but able to skip over regions.

FileOutputStream Class that writes binary data to a file. The object either overwrites a preexisting file entirely when it is constructed or appends to it. No seek or skip is possible.

Filter stream Either an input (`FilterInputStream`) or an output (`FilterOutputStream`) subclass. Filters provide additional functionality to a stream and behave as if "plugged into" the preexisting stream.

Final class A final class may not be subclassed.

Final method A final method may not be overridden.

Final variable A final variable, once initialized, may not be modified.

`finally` block A block of code that follows a `try` block and all its `catch` blocks. A `finally` block is (almost) always executed, no matter what exception is thrown or where the exception is handled.

Floating-point literal A floating-point literal either contains a decimal point, is expressed in scientific notation, or has the suffix f, F, d, or D.

Floor The floor of a number is the largest integral double value that is not greater than the number.

`FlowLayout` The default layout manager for panels and applets. This layout manager has a policy that positions components on lines in a fashion similar to the words of English text on a page.

`GridBagConstraints` The class that carries configuration information with a component to control how the component is sized and positioned by a grid bag layout.

GridBagLayout The most complex layout manager. Components are laid out in regions composed of one or more cells in an irregular grid. The width of individual columns and the height of individual rows can change when the container is resized. The changes are governed by the relative weight of each.

GridLayout This layout manager divides the container into equally sized rows and equally sized columns. Each contained component is forced to the full size of a resulting grid section.

Handler method One of the methods declared by a listener interface.

Hexadecimal literal A hex literal begins with 0x or 0X.

Identifier The name of a class, interface, method, variable, or label.

Import An import statement tells the compiler to allow the abbreviation of a fully qualified class name.

Initializer A block of code, enclosed in curly brackets, that is not part of a method. A class's initializers are executed just before constructor execution.

Inner class A class that is defined within another class.

java.lang.Runnable The interface that defines the run() method.

java.lang.Thread The class that provides the new thread of execution. Thread implements Runnable.

Label An identifier for a loop.

Labeled break Terminate execution of the labeled loop.

Labeled continue Terminate the current pass through the labeled loop.

Layout policy The rules by which a layout manager sets the size and position of components. Each layout manager has its own policy. The use of policy-based layout avoids the need for platform-dependent pixel-by-pixel specifications.

LayoutManager The interface that provides for the ability to control the size and position of components in a container.

List A collection that maintains linear order. List behavior is described by the List interface, which extends the Collection superinterface.

Listener An object that wishes to receive events of a particular category. A listener must implement the appropriate listener interface to be added to the event source.

Listener interface In the AWT, an interface that declares the handler methods for a particular category of events.

Literal string A string that appears in source code as a run of text enclosed in double quotes. Literal strings are represented by instances of java.lang.String in the literal string pool.

Literal string pool   A collection of strings that represent, without duplication, literal strings that appear in source.

Live reference   A reference that is accessible to a live thread.

Live thread   A thread that has been started but has not yet died.

Locale   The set of language, character set, and other conventions (such as currency and date presentation format) that are appropriate to a given geographical or cultural preference.

main() method   The entry point for an application.

Map   A collection that contains key/value mappings. Keys must be unique. Map behavior is described by the Map interface, which does not extend the Collection superinterface.

Mapping   An association between a key and a value.

Member variable   A variable defined within the scope of a class.

Memory leak   An area of memory that will not be used by the program but that will not be reclaimed for reuse. Java only partially protects against this problem. Write null into

references you have finished with to help yourself.

Mutator   A public method that modifies private data.

Non-runnable   The state of a thread that cannot make use of a CPU even if one is available to it. An example is a thread that is waiting for data from an I/O device.

notify()   The method in the Object class that causes a (randomly chosen) thread that is waiting on this object to be moved from the waiting state into the waiting-for-lock state.

notifyAll()   The method in the Object class that causes all threads that are waiting on this object to be moved from the waiting state into the waiting-for-lock state.

Object equality   A test for whether two possibly distinct objects are identical in the values of their important instance variables.

Object lock   The flag that is used to implement exclusivity between threads. One object lock exists for every object instance in a JVM, and each lock can be associated with either its owning object or a single thread. Note that the flag might not be "real," but it accurately describes the behavior that the JVM provides.

Octal literal   An octal literal begins with 0.

Overloading   Reuse of a method name within a class. The methods must have different argument lists and/or return types.

Overriding   Reuse of a method name in a subclass. The subclass version must have the same name, argument list, and return type as the superclass version.

Passing by value   Method arguments are copies of the values passed into the method; changes made within the method do not affect the original values.

Platform-independent file system navigation   Modern file systems can be represented as a hierarchical arrangement of files and directories based on one or more roots. However, the formats used to represent particular files in particular directories vary widely. Platform-independent file system navigation describes moving around in a file system without specific knowledge of how the paths are constructed, and is made possible by the abstractions in Java's `File` class.

Preemption   A thread-scheduling approach that depends mainly upon interactions between related threads to make the most efficient use of available CPU time.

Primitive data size   Each primitive data item has a fixed size and format when written externally by a JVM. This ensures that it is possible to take data written by one JVM on one platform and read it correctly on any other JVM on any other platform.

Private inner class   A private inner class may only be accessed from the enclosing class.

Private method   A private method may only be called by an instance of the class that owns the method.

Private variable   A private variable may only be accessed by an instance of the class that owns the variable.

Protected inner class   A protected inner class may be accessed by the enclosing class and by any subclass of the enclosing class.

Protected variable and protected method   Protected access expands on default access by allowing any subclass to read and write protected data and to call protected methods, even if the subclass is in a different package from its superclass.

Public class, protected variable, and protected method   Public access makes a feature accessible to all classes without restriction.

Public inner class   A public inner class has the same access as a protected inner class and can be more manipulated by reflection.

`public void run()`   The method declared by the `Runnable` interface. This method is the starting point for a new thread's execution.

`public void start()`   The method in the `Thread` class that launches a new thread's execution.

RandomAccessFile Class that can read and/or modify a file. This class can read and write any of the primitive types and can seek to arbitrary positions in the file.

Reader A 16-bit-wide data pipe from which Unicode text may be read.

Reference equality Tests for whether two references point to the same object.

Referenced memory Memory that is being used for storage of an object that is accessible by a live reference.

Runnable The state of a thread that can use a CPU if one is available. Nothing within the thread's state prevents it from making useful computational progress.

Runtime exception An exception that is an instance of Runtime-Exception or one of its subclasses.

Runtime type Class of an object (versus type of a reference).

Runtime.gc() A way to request garbage collection, with the same limitations as System.gc().

Set An unordered collection that does not permit duplicate elements. Set behavior is described by the Set interface, which extends the Collection superinterface.

Short-circuit operation A short-circuit operation does not evaluate its second operand if evaluation of the first operand determines the result of the operation.

Signed right shift A shift where the magnitude bits are shifted and the sign bit is extended.

sleep() A static method in the Thread class that makes the calling thread non-runnable for a specified period of time.

Static initializer A block of code, enclosed in curly brackets and pre-fixed with the static keyword, that is not part of a method. A class's static initializers are executed when the class is loaded.

Static method A static method may only access the static variables and methods of its class.

Static variable Static data belongs to its class, rather than to any instance of the class. Static variables are allocated and initialized at class-load time.

Stream An 8-bit-wide data pipe. An InputStream is a stream from which bytes may be read, and an OutputStream is one into which bytes may be written.

synchronized The keyword that indicates that prior to entering the next block, the executing thread must hold the lock on the relevant object. In the case of a synchronized instance method, the relevant object is this. In the case of a static synchronized method, the relevant object is the java.lang. Class object of the class that defines the method. In the case of a synchronized block, the relevant object is explicitly named in the argument part of the synchronized call.

System.gc()   gc() is a static method in the java.lang.System class. By calling the method, you request that the garbage collector run. However, calling the method does not guarantee that the garbage collector will run, nor does it guarantee any limiting timescale in which the garbage collector might run.

Thread scheduling   The way decisions are made about which thread will execute on a CPU at any given instant.

Threadsafe   A class that has been written in such a way that no matter how many threads execute concurrently, and how they are scheduled by the system, the data of the instances will definitely remain valid.

Time-slicing   A thread-scheduling approach that shares CPU time more or less evenly between multiple threads.

Top-level container   A frame, dialog, or window object. These containers can be made visible without being added to any other container.

try block   A block of code, prefixed with the try keyword, that might throw an exception.

Unicode   A 16-bit-wide character encoding standard. Unicode is used by all Java Virtual Machines (except Micro Edition, which is not covered by the exam) for representing text.

It represents most characters in most modern languages.

Unreferenced memory   Memory that is not being used for storage of any object accessible by a live reference.

Unsigned shift   A shift where all bits are shifted.

wait()   The method in the Object class that causes a thread to suspend execution and give up the object lock, pending notification from another thread on the same object. Often used to implement a listener behavior in a communication mechanism.

Waiting-for-lock   The state of a thread that needs to obtain the object lock to become runnable.

Weight   The element that controls how a row's height or a column's width change as the container's size changes.

Wider type   Primitive type A is wider than primitive type B if the range of A completely encompasses the range of B.

Writer   A 16-bit-wide pipe into which Unicode text may be written.

yield()   A static method in the Thread class that makes the calling thread non-runnable for an instant if other threads are runnable.

Index

SYBEX BOOKS ON THE WEB

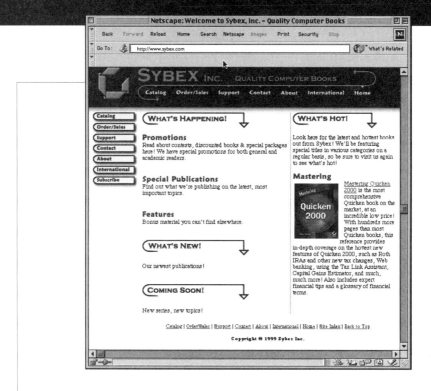

At the dynamic and informative Sybex Web site, you can:

- view our complete online catalog
- preview a book you're interested in
- access special book content
- order books online at special discount prices
- learn about Sybex

www.sybex.com

SYBEX Inc. • 1151 Marina Village Parkway
Alameda, CA 94501 • 510-523-8233

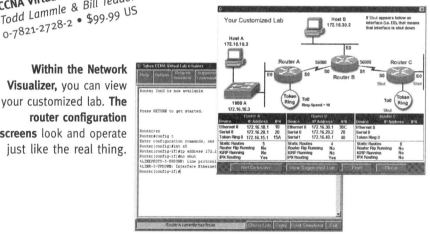

◀ continued from front

Section 6: Overloading, Overriding, Runtime Type, and Object Orientation

State the benefits of encapsulation in object-oriented design and write code that implements tightly encapsulated classes and the relationships "is a" and "has a".

Write code to invoke overridden or overloaded methods and parental or overloaded constructors; and describe the effect of invoking these methods.

Write code to construct instances of any concrete class including normal top level classes, inner classes, static inner classes, and anonymous inner classes.

Section 7: Threads

Write code to define, instantiate, and start new threads using both `java.lang.Thread` and `java.lang.Runnable`.

Recognize conditions that might prevent a thread from executing.

Write code using `synchronized, wait, notify`, or `notifyAll`, to protect against concurrent access problems and to communicate between threads. Define the interaction between threads and between threads and object locks when executing `synchronized, wait, notify`, or `notifyAll`.

Section 8: The `java.awt` Package

Write code using `component, container`, and `LayoutManager` classes of the `java.awt` package to present a GUI with specified appearance and resize behavior, and distinguish the responsibilities of layout managers from those of containers.

Write code to implement listener classes and methods, and in listener methods, extract information from the event to determine the affected component, mouse position, nature, and time of the event. State the event classname for any specified event listener interface in the `java.awt.event` package.